SELECTED REFLECTIONS
FOR THE CHRISTIAN YEAR

NICK FAWCETT

kevin mayhew

kevin mayhew

First published in Great Britain in 2014 by Kevin Mayhew Ltd
Buxhall, Stowmarket, Suffolk IP14 3BW
Tel: +44 (0) 1449 737978 Fax: +44 (0) 1449 737834
E-mail: info@kevinmayhew.com

www.kevinmayhew.com

© Copyright 2014 Nick Fawcett.

The right of Nick Fawcett to be identified as the author of this work has been asserted by him in accordance with the Copyright, Designs and Patents Act 1988.

The publishers wish to thank all those who have given their permission to reproduce copyright material in this publication.

Every effort has been made to trace the owners of copyright material and we hope that no copyright has been infringed. Pardon is sought and apology made if the contrary be the case, and a correction will be made in any reprint of this book.

All rights reserved. No part of this publication may be reproduced, stored in a retrieval system, or transmitted, in any form or by any means, electronic, mechanical, photocopying, recording, or otherwise, without the prior written permission of the publisher.

All Scripture quotations are translated or paraphrased by Nick Fawcett.

9 8 7 6 5 4 3 2 1 0

ISBN 978 1 84867 743 2
Catalogue No. 1501457

Cover design by Rob Mortonson
© Images used under licence from Shutterstock Inc.
Typeset by Richard Weaver

Printed and bound in Great Britain

Contents

About the author		10
Introduction		11

Advent

1st week in Advent

1	Zephaniah 1:12-16	*Called to account*	14
2	Malachi 2:17–3:3a, 5	*An unwelcome surprise*	16
3	Matthew 24:36, 44	*Ready and waiting*	18
4	Matthew 25:31-40	*The litmus test of faith*	20
5	Mark 1:15	*Glimpsing the kingdom*	22
6	Mark 13:31, 32	*End times?*	24
7	Luke 9:26	*Declaring our allegiance*	26
8	Romans 13:11	*Rise and shine*	28
9	2 Peter 3:9, 10a, 11b, 12a, 13, 14	*All in good time*	30

2nd week in Advent

10	Isaiah 40:3a	*Prepared for what?*	32
11	Isaiah 40:3b	*Make straight his way*	34
12	Matthew 11:2-5	*Keeping faith*	36
13	Mark 1:4	*Ready to change?*	38
14	Luke 1:11-15a, 18-20	*Believing the impossible*	40
15	Luke 1:16, 17	*Preparing the way*	42
16	Luke 1:67, 68	*A time for worship*	44
17	Luke 1:78, 79	*The rising sun*	46
18	John 1:6-8	*Pointing the way*	48
19	1 Thessalonians 5:1-10	*Be prepared*	50

3rd week in Advent

20	Isaiah 1:18	*As white as snow*	52
21	Isaiah 46:9, 10, 11b	*God's active word*	54
22	Isaiah 52:7, 8a	*A time for rejoicing*	56
23	Matthew 1:1-6	*Unlikely choices*	58

24	Matthew 1:21, 22	*Fulfilment in Christ*	60
25	Matthew 2:5b	*God's living word*	62
26	Matthew 6:10	*Thy kingdom come*	64
27	Luke 4:18, 19	*A time to give*	66
28	1 Timothy 2:5, 6	*Giving his all*	68

4th week in Advent

29	Isaiah 11:6-9	*Vision for the future*	70
30	Micah 5:2-5a	*From small beginnings*	72
31	Luke 1:26-35	*Who? Me!*	74
32	Luke 1:38	*Ready to say yes*	76
33	Luke 1:46-49	*Magnifying the Lord*	78
34	Luke 1:51-53	*Beyond the margins*	80
35	Luke 1:54, 55	*Faithful to his promise*	82
36	Luke 1:67, 68a, 72-75	*From fear to love*	84
37	John 1:1-3a	*The start of it all*	86
38	John 1:10, 11	*The forgotten person?*	88
39	John 3:16	*The God who believes in us!*	90
40	John 12:46	*The God who comes to us*	92
41	Galatians 4:4, 5	*The fullness of time*	94

Christmas

42	Isaiah 9:2	*Light of the world*	98
43	Matthew 1:18-20	*Ready and willing*	100
44	Matthew 1:21, 24, 25	*Who? Them!*	102
45	Matthew 1:22, 23	*Truly with us*	104
46	Luke 1:34, 35	*Life-changing power*	106
47	Luke 2:1-5	*In heart and mind*	108
48	Luke 2:6, 7	*Making room*	110
49	Luke 2:8, 9	*Ordinary people*	112
50	Luke 2:10, 11	*Good news!*	114
51	Luke 2:12-14	*It is you!*	116
52	Luke 2:15	*Seeing for ourselves*	118
53	Luke 2:16	*Something worth hurrying for*	120
54	Luke 2:17, 18	*Something worth sharing*	122
55	Luke 2:19	*Digging deeper*	124

56	Luke 2:25-33a	*Keeping faith*	126
57	Luke 2:34, 35	*A costly response*	128
58	John 1:3b, 4	*Something beautiful for him*	130
59	John 1:10, 11	*An unwanted gift*	132
60	John 1:12, 13	*RSVP*	134
61	John 1:14	*My word!*	136
62	Hebrews 1:1-3a; 2:1	*A continuing response*	138
63	Hebrews 2:14a	*One with us*	140

New Year's Eve

64	Psalm 89:1, 2	*Great is his faithfulness*	144
65	John 20:30, 31	*The message that speaks for itself*	146

New Year's Day

66	Psalm 90:1-4, 10, 12	*Time's paces*	150
67	Ecclesiastes 11:7	*The time of our life*	152

Epiphany

68	Matthew 2:1, 2	*Wise men still seek him*	156
69	Matthew 2:3, 4	*A mixed response*	158
70	Matthew 2:7, 8	*A careful search*	160
71	Matthew 2:9, 10	*Never too late*	162
72	Matthew 2:11b, 12	*Which way now?*	164

Week of Prayer for Christian Unity

73	Psalm 133:1-3	*Living in peace*	168
74	Luke 9:49, 50	*One people?*	170
75	1 Corinthians 1:10	*An unbreakable bond*	172
76	1 Corinthians 12:12, 15-20	*Celebrating our diversity*	174
77	Ephesians 2:19-21	*United we stand*	176

Shrove Tuesday

78	Psalm 32:1-5	*Something to celebrate?*	180

Lent

Temptation, self-examination and forgiveness

79	Genesis 3:9-13	*Original sin?*	184
80	Psalm 19:12	*Forgive our faults*	186
81	Psalm 26:2, 3	*Examination time?*	188
82	Psalm 38:18	*I'm so sorry!*	190
83	Psalm 51:2, 7	*Washed clean*	192
84	Psalm 69:5	*An unwitting mistake*	194
85	Psalm 103:8-12	*Undeserved pardon*	196
86	Proverbs 28:13	*A clean breast of it*	198
87	Jeremiah 2:22	*Made clean*	200
88	Micah 7:18, 19	*The true picture*	202
89	Matthew 3:1, 2	*Changing course*	204
90	Matthew 4:1-4	*A tempting prospect*	206
91	2 Corinthians 13:5	*Taking stock*	208
92	James 3:2a	*A second chance*	210

Sacrifice and self-denial

93	Proverbs 14:21, 31	*Sharing our plenty*	212
94	Matthew 5:40-42	*That little bit extra*	214
95	Matthew 6:16-18	*Parading our virtue*	216
96	Matthew 6:19-21	*Lasting treasure*	218
97	Luke 9:23, 24	*The cost of discipleship*	220
98	Colossians 2:20–3:2	*A positive response*	222

Stillness and quietness

99	Genesis 2:2	*Take a break*	224
100	Psalm 39:5	*What's the hurry?*	226
101	Ecclesiastes 3:1-8	*A time and a place*	228
102	Ecclesiastes 4:6	*Quiet contentment*	230
103	Isaiah 30:15	*Slow down*	232
104	Matthew 14:22, 23	*A time to be still*	234
105	Mark 6:31	*A quiet place*	236
106	Mark 6:45, 46	*Stepping back, stepping forward*	238
107	Luke 10:40-42	*A pause for thought*	240

Spiritual growth

108	Psalm 92:12-14	*Freshening up*	242

109	Proverbs 1:5-7	*Words of wisdom*	244
110	Isaiah 55:1, 2	*Food for our souls*	246
111	Hosea 6:3	*Keep moving*	248
112	Mark 8:29-33	*An evolving faith*	250
113	1 Corinthians 3:2, 3a	*Tuck in*	252
114	1 Corinthians 13:11	*Growing up*	254
115	Ephesians 4:11-14a, 15	*Pot-bound Christians*	256
116	Jude v. 20	*Build yourselves up*	258

The Transfiguration

117	Mark 9:2-4	*A glimpse of glory*	260
118	Luke 9:29, 30, 32, 33	*Letting go*	262

Holy Week

Palm Sunday

119	Mark 11:7-10	*A royal welcome*	266
120	Luke 19:36-42	*Changing our tune*	268

Holy Monday to Wednesday

121	Mark 10:32	*One step beyond*	270
122	Mark 11:15	*Totally devoted to you!*	272
123	Luke 9:23, 24	*Taking up our cross*	274
124	Luke 22:8-13	*Unsung disciples*	276
125	1 Corinthians 1:18, 23, 24	*Conveying what message?*	278

Maundy Thursday

126	Matthew 26:21, 22	*Constant to the end*	280
127	Matthew 26:28, 29	*Giving blood*	282
128	Mark 14:22-25	*Look both ways*	284
129	Mark 14:32-36	*The valley of tears*	286
130	Mark 14:51, 52	*A changed life?*	288
131	John 13:6-9, 12, 14-16	*Ready to serve*	290
132	John 13:36-38	*All talk?*	292

Good Friday

133	Matthew 26:69-71	*A changed man*	294
134	Mark 15:29-32a	*A straight choice*	296
135	Mark 15:34	*The ultimate sacrifice*	298

136	Luke 23:44, 45a	*God in the darkness*	300
137	John 19:38-40	*Secret disciples?*	302
138	Romans 5:6-8	*Precious to him*	304

Easter Eve
| 139 | Mark 15:43-47 | *Dealing with death* | 306 |
| 140 | John 19:31-34a | *He was dead* | 308 |

Easter

141	Matthew 27:62-66	*The God who cannot be kept down*	312
142	Matthew 28:11-14	*The truth that couldn't be hidden*	314
143	Matthew 28:15a	*Truth will out!*	316
144	Matthew 28:16-20	*Still good news*	318
145	Luke 24:5b	*From defeat to victory*	320
146	Luke 24:9-11	*Too good to be true?*	322
147	Luke 24:13-21a	*The road to life*	324
148	Luke 24:22-27	*Better than expected*	326
149	Luke 24:28-32	*Light up the fire*	328
150	John 20:11-16	*Beginnings from endings*	330
151	John 20:17, 18	*A taste of Eden*	332
152	John 20:19, 20	*A world-changing event*	334
153	John 20:27-29	*Beyond doubt*	336
154	John 21:15-17	*A second chance*	338
155	1 Corinthians 15:35	*The assurance of things hoped for*	340
156	1 Corinthians 15:51-53	*Resurrection promise*	342
157	1 Corinthians 15:54b-57	*Over and done with*	344
158	Ephesians 5:14b	*Son rise*	346
159	Colossians 1:3-6	*Making waves*	348
160	1 Peter 1:3, 4	*We've only just begun*	350

Ascension Day

| 161 | Acts 1:6-11 | *The complete picture* | 354 |
| 162 | Philippians 2:9-11 | *Glimpsing Christ's glory* | 356 |

Pentecost

| 163 | Zechariah 4:6 | *No contest!* | 360 |

164	Matthew 28:18, 19	*Standby Christians*	362
165	Acts 2:1-4, 16-18a	*A gift for all*	364
166	2 Corinthians 3:17	*Gloriously free*	366
167	Romans 8:26, 27	*Partners in prayer*	368
168	1 John 3:24b	*With him in Spirit*	370

Trinity Sunday

169	John 16:12-15	*The complete picture*	374
170	1 Corinthians 12:4-6	*A glorious mystery*	376

Harvest

171	Genesis 1:26	*Caring for God's world*	380
172	Psalm 24:1; 95:4	*The call to conserve*	382
173	Psalm 95:3-7a	*Stewards of creation*	384
174	Hosea 8:7a; 10:12a	*Consider what you sow*	386
175	Mark 4:2-9	*An unlikely harvest*	388
176	Galatians 5:22	*Spring blossom*	390
177	Galatians 6:7-9	*Reaping what we sow*	392

All Saints' Day

178	Philippians 3:17	*A rare breed*	396
179	Hebrews 12:1, 2	*Running together*	398
180	Hebrews 13:5	*All saints*	400

Remembrance Day

181	Psalm 44:1, 7a	*Lest we forget*	404
182	John 15:13	*A debt owed*	406

Index of biblical passages   409

About the author

Brought up in Southend-in-Sea, Essex, Nick Fawcett trained for the Baptist ministry at Bristol and Oxford, before serving churches in Lancashire and Cheltenham. He subsequently spent three years as a chaplain with the Christian movement Toc H, before focusing on writing and editing, which he continues with today, despite wrestling with myeloma, a currently incurable cancer of the bone marrow. He lives with his wife, Deborah, and two children – Samuel and Kate – in Wellington, Somerset, worshipping, when able, at the local Anglican church. A keen walker, he delights in the beauty of the Somerset and Devon countryside around his home, his numerous books owing much to the inspiration he unfailingly finds there.

Nick has had over 130 books published by Kevin Mayhew. For details, please refer to our website: www.kevinmayhew.com

Introduction

Some passages of the Bible stand out in the memory, don't they? And that's especially so when it comes to key Christian seasons such as Advent, Christmas, Holy Week or Easter. Who can forget the words of Luke concerning the Annunciation to Mary; of Matthew concerning the journey of the magi; of John concerning the Word made flesh. Who can forget the testimony of each of the Gospel writers to Jesus' agonising in Gethsemane or his suffering and death on a cross. And who can forget, equally, the outpourings of joy, wonder and amazement in the resurrection narratives as the risen Christ appeared to his followers. The words of Scripture concerning events such as these have encouraged, comforted, strengthened and inspired Christians across the centuries, becoming so familiar to us that we greet them each year almost like old friends. The problem is that they may become over-familiar, to the point that they no longer speak to us as they once did. The words wash over us without really hitting home, such that we find it harder and harder to take in what we are reading or hearing.

In this compilation I've sought to address that problem by carefully adapting material from my two daily devotionals (*Daily Prayer* and *Daily Prayer 2*) to offer brief reflections on key passages relating to the seasons of the Christian year and other events in the Church calendar. There are sessions here for each week of Advent, as well as for Shrove Tuesday and the forty days of Lent. There's material for Christmas, Holy Week and Easter, as well as other key seasons, and I've supplemented these with thoughts for New Year's Eve, New Year's Day and other dates in the Church year. Inevitably, I've had to omit some passages I might have chosen, but hopefully those I've selected – each supplemented by a simple closing prayer – will help to bring home afresh the awesome riches of the good news of Christ that the Christian seasons and Church calendar so wonderfully and succinctly encapsulate.

Nick Fawcett

ADVENT

FIRST WEEK IN ADVENT

1
Zephaniah 1:12-16
Called to account

At that time I will search Jerusalem with a lantern, and I will punish those who sit smugly over the last of their wine, assuring themselves, 'The Lord won't do anything to us, either good or bad.' Their wealth shall be plundered, and their homes laid waste. Though they build houses, they will never live in them; though they plant vineyards, they will drink no wine from them. The great day of the Lord draws near, rushing ever closer upon us; the sound of that day will be bitter, and the warrior will cry aloud there. It will be a day of wrath, of misery and hardship, ruin and desolation – a day of clouds and thick darkness, of trumpet blast and battle cry against the fortified cities and lofty battlements.

Reflection

The older one gets, the more one comes to recognise that life isn't fair. The heady idealism of youth gives way to the hard-headed realism of middle age, as the truth slowly dawns that, in this life at least, people don't always get what they deserve. Honesty may be the best policy when it comes to peace of mind, but it is not necessarily the most lucrative; the unpleasant truth is that all too often cheats *do* prosper.

Coming to terms with facts like this is a painful business and one that can test faith to the limit, just as it did in the time of Zephaniah. There were many in his day who, faced by the apparent injustices of life, concluded that God was either disinterested in human affairs or powerless to intervene. It was an understandable mistake, but one that the prophet had no time for. In God's time, he warns, justice will be done, and seen to be done by all. We lose sight of that at our peril.

Prayer

Sovereign God,
    day after day I see so much that is wrong,
    so much that I cannot make sense of,
    and I ask myself why you stand by and let it happen.
I watch helplessly as truth is trodden underfoot,
    love exploited,
    and the innocent suffer,
    while those who least deserve it seem to flourish.
Help me, confronted by such puzzles, not to lose heart.
Teach me to recognise that loving you brings its own rewards,
    greater than any this world can offer,
    and remind me also that the time will come when everyone will answer to you,
    and justice will prevail.
Amen.

2
Malachi 2:17–3:3a, 5

An unwelcome surprise

You have exhausted the Lord with all your talk, yet you ask, 'In what way have we wearied him?' By claiming that those who do evil are good in the sight of the Lord, and that he takes pleasure in them, and by asking, 'Where is the God of justice?' 'Look,' says the Lord of hosts, 'I am sending my messenger to prepare the way for me, so that the Lord whom you seek will suddenly come to his temple. The messenger of the covenant whom you so eagerly anticipate is coming, but who can endure the day of his coming or stand when he appears? For he is like a refiner's fire and fullers' soap; he will preside as a refiner and purifier of silver, and he will purify the descendants of Levi. I will approach you in judgement, and be swift to bear witness against the sorcerers, the adulterers and those who bear false witness; against those who exploit their hired workers, the widow and the orphan, who thrust aside the alien, and who do not fear me,' says the Lord of hosts.

Reflection

Anyone who has ever listened to Handel's *Messiah* will be familiar with those words of the prophet Malachi. They make sobering reading, not least because those to whom they were first addressed were convinced they were more than ready to welcome God's promised deliverer, and assured of his approval when he came. From Malachi came the call to think again – a warning that the day of the Lord would be anything but welcome. Why? Because their lives were a pale shadow of what the Messiah would expect from them. Their expectation of God's blessing had become divorced from their day-to-day existence, and the result, warned the prophet, would be an unpleasant shock.

There is a danger that we today can make the same mistake. We may believe that we are ready to face God's judgement, whenever and however that may come, but before we sit back complacently we would do well to examine our consciences, assess our lifestyles and ask whether everything in our life is quite as it should be. Fail to do that, and we may find the day of the Lord not quite the occasion we like to imagine.

Prayer

Lord Jesus Christ,
    I talk of listening to *your* voice,
    but I hear what *I* want to hear.
I speak of seeking *your* will,
    yet I prefer *my* way,
    expecting you to conform to *my* expectations.
Save me from a life that proclaims one thing, but displays another.
Prepare me for your coming again,
    so that I may be ready to receive you
    and found faithful in your service.
Amen.

3
Matthew 24:36, 44
Ready and waiting

'No one knows the details concerning that day and hour, not even the angels in heaven or the Son; only the Father. So, then, you need to be ready, for when the Son of Man comes it will be at an hour you do not expect.'

Reflection

From time immemorial, people have wanted to see into the future, and plenty have claimed to do just that, whether through studying the stars, gazing into a crystal ball, inspecting a chicken's entrails or swirling tea leaves in a cup. Generally, our own attempts are less ambitious, ranging perhaps from forecasting eight score draws or six jackpot numbers to gauging mortgage rates, pondering employment prospects and planning for retirement. Then, of course, there are the professionals: weather forecasters, financial gurus, political pollsters and pundits, scientists warning of global warming and environmental catastrophes, economic analysts, stock market investors and so forth – each, to the best of their ability, reading the signs and acting accordingly.

The Church, too, has got in on the act, many across the years having confidently announced that the last days are upon us, and though each has been proved wrong, no doubt many others will speculate likewise in the years ahead. But should we really be reading between the lines of current events, searching for signs of Christ's return? On the face of it, Advent seems to suggest yes, its concern with end times encapsulated by the traditional refrain, 'Come, Lord, come'. But, as Jesus warned his followers on more than one occasion, 'No one knows the details concerning that day or hour.' It's not *when* the kingdom might come that matters, nor even ultimately that it *will*, but the fact that it has already dawned, inaugurated in Christ's birth and ministry and brought nearer by his victory over death. Unrecognised, perhaps, indiscernible to most, but to the eye of faith it's here already. True, the fulfilment is yet to come, a day when Christ will rule on earth as in heaven, but we are called to celebrate his love *now*, taste his joy *now*, seek his mercy *now* and offer our service *now*. Trust in the future, yes; anticipate it, certainly; prepare for it, without question; but do so by focusing on the response you make in the present – and leave the rest to him.

Prayer

Eternal God,
   help me to know you now,
   love you now,
   serve you now –
   to live each day as your child,
   seeking and honouring your will.
Open my heart to the reality of your kingdom here on earth
   and teach me more of your way,
   so that in everything I do, think and say
   I may work to help it grow,
   bringing your purpose to fruition.
Amen.

4
Matthew 25:31-40

The litmus test of faith

'When the Son of Man comes in his glory, together with his angels, he will sit in state on his throne, with all the nations gathered before him, and he will separate people one from the other as a shepherd separates the sheep from the goats, putting the sheep to his right and the goats to his left. Then the king will say to those on his right, "Come, those who my Father has blessed – inherit the kingdom prepared for you from the foundation of the world. I was hungry and you gave me something to eat, thirsty and you gave me a drink, a stranger and you made me welcome, naked and you clothed me, sick and you visited me, in prison and you had time for me." Then the righteous will answer, "Lord, when did we see you hungry and give you food, or thirsty and give you a drink? When did we see you a stranger and make you welcome, or naked and clothe you? When was it that we saw you sick or in prison and visited you?" Then the king will answer, "I tell you the truth, whenever you did it to the least of your brothers and sisters, you did it also to me."'

Reflection

Do you remember your first chemistry experiment at school? Almost certainly it involved a piece of litmus paper, dipped into a test-tube of liquid to see if it turned red or blue, indicating acid or alkali. There is something of that experiment in the words of Jesus concerning the sheep and the goats, only this time the test concerns something very different – how faithfully we have responded to Christ.

What are the distinguishing features we should look for? Doctrinal soundness? Faith that can move mountains? Gifts of the Spirit? An impeccable record of church attendance? Not according to this parable, they're not. What counts, rather, is whether we have responded to people in need; whether we have shown our faith in action, expressing through our care and compassion the love of Christ. That, we are told, is the litmus test of Christian discipleship. Of course, we need to consider such words in the light of Christ's teaching concerning mercy and forgiveness, but we should not use that to evade or tone down their challenge. Faith may not depend on works but it ought to result in them, at least in part. The warning here is not so much that Jesus will reject us but that, through turning our back on others, we may find that *we* have rejected *him*.

Prayer

Lord Jesus Christ,
> I turn serving you into a matter of private devotion and personal fulfilment,
> tailoring the gospel to suit my own ends
> rather than allowing it to shape my life.

Forgive me for being so preoccupied with heaven that I forget needs here on earth,
> for focusing too much on myself and too little on others.

Teach me that, though I can never earn my salvation,
> I need to show the reality of my faith through the way I live.

Grant, then, that my deeds may speak as clearly as my words,
> my whole life testifying to your love.

Amen.

5
Mark 1:15

Glimpsing the kingdom

'The time is fulfilled, and the kingdom of God has come near.'

Reflection

'Much of what we see depends on what we are looking for.' In other words, we often miss something that is staring us in the face, either because we are closed to the possibility of seeing it or because we are preoccupied with something else. Jesus was aware of that problem, his use of parables being designed to break through people's preconceptions so that they might see the world in a new light.

That need is as real today as ever, especially when it comes to understanding the kingdom of God. All too easily, we relegate that kingdom to some far-off place and time. Certainly, the final consummation of God's purpose must come later, but, as Jesus proclaimed at the very start of his ministry, 'The time is fulfilled, and the kingdom of God has come near' (Mark 1:15). The fact is that the kingdom has already dawned, if only we have eyes to see it. Like yeast or a mustard seed, it is slowly growing, its presence evidenced in countless lives being changed every day, in numerous expressions of love and service, in the work and worship of the Church, and in so much more. As well, then, as looking to the future and praying 'Come, Lord, come', we need to nurture the seeds that Jesus has already sown, ensuring we do all in our power, through his grace, to see them grow.

Prayer

Gracious God,
> teach me that your kingdom is not confined to the distant future,
> but in a real sense is already present here and now.

Inspire me through all those who have caught a vision of that truth,
> and all who have had the faith and dedication to translate that
> vision into reality.

Help me to learn from them
> and to offer you my service, as best I may,
> working with your people everywhere to see your will done
> and your kingdom come in all its glory.

Amen.

6
Mark 13:31, 32

End times?

'Unlike heaven and earth, which will end, my words will never pass away. But as to the day or hour that this world will end, nobody except the Father knows it, not even the angels in heaven or the Son.'

Reflection

I wrote this reflection in a hurry, for, according to a preacher from Oakland, California, the end of the world was just around the corner: to be exact, at 6pm the following day. Actually, of course, I was in no hurry at all, for I pay no credence whatsoever to such drivel. People have been predicting the end of the world with depressing regularity since time immemorial, and no doubt they will continue to do so for years to come, which is all very strange when you consider the words of Jesus above, in which he makes it quite clear that nobody but God knows when the end times will be. Elsewhere, he stresses that we should not concern ourselves with such things, but instead get on with the daily business of life and service.

Certainly we are called to look forward to his coming again and to ensure that we are ready to greet him when he does. But when that will be, where and how it will happen, what it will involve and so forth are not for us to concern ourselves with. What Jesus was saying to his disciples is that, come what may, we must keep faith. Heaven and earth may pass away, and so too may we, but though *this* life may end, our hope is in things unseen, a kingdom beyond this world. That's what matters: faith in the future shaping the present, so that instead of fretting about what's to come we live now as he would wish. Don't brood on tomorrow. Rejoice today, and trust in him. We may pass *on* before he comes, but, like his words, we will never pass *away*.

Prayer

Almighty God,
>thank you for giving me joy in the present
>and hope for the future;
>for the sure and certain knowledge that your love not only surrounds me now,
>but will continue to do so for all eternity,
>nothing in heaven or earth,
>life or death,
>being able to separate me from it.

Deepen my faith in everything you hold in store,
>and may that assurance shape every aspect of who and what I am.

Amen.

7
Luke 9:26

Declaring our allegiance

'Anyone who is ashamed of me and my words, the Son of Man will be ashamed of in turn when he comes in his glory and the glory of the Father and the holy angels.'

Reflection

I toyed in my youth with buying a T-shirt, sweater or scarf in the colours of my favourite football team, but always in the end decided against it. Partly, perhaps, that was down to my team's fluctuating fortunes, but the main reason was that I preferred to be incognito in case I should find myself surrounded by rival supporters. In ordinary clothes I could blend in with the crowd and melt away from trouble; with my colours nailed to the mast it would be much harder. Though it was unlikely I'd be set upon, better safe than sorry.

It's highly improbable that we'll ever encounter aggression on account of our faith, most people being apathetic rather than hostile towards Christianity, but are we ready nonetheless to be identified with Christ? Though we wouldn't want to ram religion down people's throats or trumpet our commitment, our allegiance should surely be plain to all. Is that true of us, or do we prefer to keep our faith hidden, feeling slightly embarrassed to talk about it, even to admit we go to church? Yes, we might fairly fight shy of certain stereotypes, but never confuse those with what being a Christian is ultimately all about. Never be ashamed of Christ, or the time may come when you find him ashamed of you.

Prayer

Father God,
   forgive me, for sometimes,
   afraid of being pigeonholed or associated with stereotypes,
   I conceal my commitment to you and keep quiet about my faith.
Instead of worrying about the impression some Christians may
   give of you,
   or the preconceptions others might have,
   may I live in such a way as to show what you mean to *me*
   and to make my gratitude, love and allegiance clear to all.
Amen.

8
Romans 13:11

Rise and shine

You are well aware of the times we're living in. It's high time for you to awake, for the day of our salvation is closer than when we first came to faith.

Reflection

Few of us like getting up in the morning, but of course we have to, and for those who need to rise early an alarm clock is essential, it being the only thing guaranteed to arouse them from their slumber in readiness for another day. I had an alarm clock once that was particularly special. Bought for me by my wife at Christmas many years back, it featured a photograph of my two children and a recorded message from them both. What better sight and sound could I have asked for to wake up to? Though I still groaned with dismay when the alarm went off, my reluctance to wake up was tempered by their well-loved voices.

Advent offers an alarm clock of a different sort. Far more than a prelude to Christmas, it reminds us of the central themes of the gospel – of what God has done, is doing and will yet do – and as such it serves as an annual wake-up call to hear and respond. The above words of Paul to the Romans perfectly capture that sense of urgency: 'awake, for the day of our salvation is closer than when we first came to faith'. Here, in other words, is a summons to rouse ourselves and hear again the message of Christ; to shake off our lethargy and commit ourselves afresh to his service. Do we still hear his voice and answer his call? Or have we metaphorically rolled over and dozed off in our discipleship? Take time, this Advent, to read again the Gospels and to reflect on what they say to you. Take time to listen and to hear God speaking through them.

Prayer

Loving God,
> I like to imagine that my commitment is as vibrant as it's always been,
> but I know that it's not.

I like to think that when you call I'm swift to hear and eager to answer,
> but the truth is rather different.

My discipleship is constantly under attack,
> not just from temptation but equally through lethargy and complacency.

Rouse me to your wake-up call,
> your summons to faith.

Speak your word,
> and help me to respond in repentance, commitment and service,
> resolved to serve you more faithfully each and every day.

Amen.

9
2 Peter 3:9, 10a, 11b, 12a, 13, 14

All in good time

Despite what some may imagine, the Lord is not slow to honour his promise. Rather, he is showing patience towards you, wanting everyone to turn from their sins rather than be destroyed. The day of the Lord will steal upon you like a thief. So then, as you wait for that day to dawn, consecrate your lives as holy to God and strive to bring it here sooner. We wait for a new heaven and earth, just as God has promised, where righteousness will feel at home. As you anticipate that day, my friends, do everything in your power to remain pure and blameless in God's sight, at one with him.

Reflection

A watched kettle, they say, never boils, which of course is another way of saying that the longer we wait for something the longer it seems to take in coming. Twenty minutes waiting for a bus or train can feel more like twenty hours. Weeks waiting for a hospital appointment or for news concerning the outcome of treatment can seem an eternity. Likewise, if we're eagerly looking forward to something, time can seem to pass frustratingly slowly.

The lesson is simple: don't waste your time counting down the minutes, days, weeks or months before an anticipated event. Get on with the day-to-day business of living, assured that the day you are waiting for will come. And if that's true of little things – birthdays or holidays, for example – it's true all the more of the expectation at the heart of Advent: the promised return of Christ. Should we look forward to that day? Yes. Should it dominate our thinking? No, or at least not in the sense of dwelling and speculating on end times. The whys and wherefores of his coming are not for us to know. We are called simply to trust that, in his own time, Jesus will return to establish his kingdom, and in the meantime to live in such a way that, whenever he comes, we're ready and happy to greet him.

Prayer

Lord Jesus Christ,
> save me from losing faith in the ultimate fulfilment of your purpose –
> in your promise to return and establish your kingdom.

Teach me to live each day in the light of your tomorrow;
> not as though you *may* return
> but in the knowledge that,
> through your Spirit,
> you are here already,
> and that one day I will meet you face to face.

Amen.

SECOND WEEK IN ADVENT

10

Isaiah 40:3a

Prepared for what?

A voice proclaims: 'Prepare the Lord's way in the desert.'

Reflection

'Here's one I prepared earlier' – words made famous by the children's TV programme *Blue Peter*. The catchphrase became so familiar that, even today, its very mention is guaranteed to raise a smile. Of course, the importance of being prepared can scarcely be overemphasised. Imagine being operated on by an untrained surgeon, or entering a marathon without months of training, or sitting an exam without first revising, or listening to a sermon delivered off the cuff. In countless areas of life, if we're not prepared then we or others will suffer the consequences. Hence, another catchphrase, immortalised as the Boy Scout motto: 'Be prepared'.

That, in a nutshell, is the message of Advent. But prepared for what? Despite what the hustle and bustle associated with this time of year may tell you, these few weeks are not just about getting ready for Christmas – writing cards, buying presents, stocking up with food, hanging decorations and so forth. Rather, they're about ensuring we're ready to meet Jesus should he come again, about honouring and serving him in our lives, about hearing his call and glimpsing his presence in the world around us. Just as the surgeon goes on learning, the athlete goes on training, the student goes on revising and the preacher goes on studying, so discipleship involves ongoing development. It calls for faithfulness in prayer and worship, in reflecting on the message and meaning of Christ, in consecrating our time and gifts to God, in examining ourselves to ensure we are still walking in faith. It means, in short, ensuring that we remain ready and willing to walk the Christian way. Whoever we are, none of us is as ready as we like to think. Advent offers us the opportunity to take stock, to reflect and to respond.

Prayer

Redeemer God,
>   prepare me to worship you:
>   to recognise your love, mercy, purpose and power
>   and to offer my heartfelt praise.

Prepare me to serve you:
>   to understand your will and respond to your calling,
>   consecrating my life to the growth of your kingdom in thought,
>   word and deed.

Prepare me to know you:
>   to learn more of your goodness, truth and nature,
>   your work in human history across the years.

Prepare me to welcome you:
>   to live each day, each moment, in the light of your promises,
>   ready to welcome my Saviour Christ when he comes again
>   in glory.

Make straight a highway in the wilderness of my life,
>   so that he may work in and through me,
>   by your grace.

Amen.

11
Isaiah 40:3b

Make straight his way

'... make ready in the wilderness a straight highway along which our God can come.'

Reflection

Drive down many of the roads near my home, situated along the Devon/Somerset border, and you can be sure it will involve numerous twists and turns. It's a decidedly rural part of the country, characterised by narrow and frequently tortuous country lanes that weave their way between farmsteads up hills and down valleys. Going any distance along them can take a considerable time. But there's one road which, although it's marked on the map as a lane, is a delight to drive on – long and almost arrow-straight for the best part of seven miles. It is, as you'll no doubt have guessed, an old Roman road, and every time I go down it I marvel at the skill of those Roman road-builders centuries ago. They certainly knew how to get from A to B as quickly as possible. They had their reasons, of course – partly it was to facilitate trade and partly to ensure that their armies could swiftly respond to any whiff of trouble, but the benefits of their foresight continue to be enjoyed even today.

John the Baptist, of course – the voice in the wilderness, fulfilling the words of the prophet Isaiah – spoke of making straight a very different kind of road: a highway into the wilderness of human lives for the coming of Christ. His listeners, who flocked out into the wilderness to hear him, believed they were more than ready to welcome him, but they were in for a rude awakening as John spoke of the wrath to come and trees failing to bear fruit, leaving them in no doubt as to who he had in mind.

Prepare yourselves, said John, before it's too late. Ensure that the way is clear for Jesus to enter into your lives. The challenge applies as much to us today.

Prayer

Lord Jesus Christ,
  promised of old,
  foretold by prophets,
  long awaited by your people,
  prepare a way in my heart so that you may more fully enter in.
Saviour Christ,
  rejected and despised,
  nailed to a cross and sealed in a tomb,
  break down the barriers of doubt and disbelief that keep me from you –
  the faults and failings that deny your love and obstruct your purpose.
Risen Christ,
  here through your Spirit,
  here by my side,
  fill me with your love,
  redeem me by your grace
  and renew me by your power.
Sovereign Christ,
  coming to redeem your people,
  to reign in glory and to welcome me into your kingdom,
  make your path straight within me,
  so that, consecrated to your service,
  I in turn may help to prepare your way in the lives of others.
Amen.

12
Matthew 11:2-5

Keeping faith

When John heard in prison what the Messiah was doing, he sent word by his disciples and said to him, 'Are you the one who is to come, or are we to wait for another?' Jesus answered them, 'Go and tell John what you hear and see: the blind receive their sight, the lame walk, the lepers are cleansed, the deaf hear, the dead are raised, and the poor have good news brought to them.'

Reflection

Christmas crackers are invariably disappointing, aren't they? They look so full of promise stacked neatly in the box, but when you come to pull them it's always to find the same old tat inside. They're all show and no substance. And that sense of anti-climax rather describes how John the Baptist must have felt as he languished in prison following his arrest by Herod. He'd begun his ministry full of anticipation, believing that the kingdom of God was at hand, but now he found himself confined to a prison cell. Understandably, he started to question, wondering if God was at work in Christ after all. If so, why was Herod still in control? Why did evil continue to prosper? Why did nothing appear to have changed?

We can feel the same, when we look at our world. Has anything really changed for the better? Have *we* changed? Is the gospel really able to make a difference to life, or is it simply wishful thinking? For John, the answer came in reports concerning Jesus. Despite the fact that he, too, was experiencing hostility and rejection, people were being transformed by his touch – healed, renewed, restored, forgiven. Yes, there was still evil, injustice, sorrow and suffering, but the kingdom of God was nonetheless starting to grow. And, for all that remains wrong in the world today, lives continue to be changed. In peace discovered, hope reborn, strength gained, love shown, faith kindled, joy experienced and meaning found, God continues to bring new beginnings in Christ. Keep faith, for despite everything that frustrates his purpose and obscures his love, he is still at work, and the kingdom is growing among us.

Prayer

Loving God,
> teach me to see not just the bad in the world
> but also the good,
> not only that which denies your love
> but also that which speaks of it and testifies to your
> transforming grace.

Despite everything that seems to deny your love and frustrate
> your purpose,
> help me to keep faith in your renewing power and
> redeeming love,
> in the signs of your kingdom here on earth,
> as it is in heaven.

Amen.

13
Mark 1:4

Ready to change?

John the baptiser appeared in the desert, calling for baptism as a sign of repentance and the forgiveness of sins.

Reflection

A few years ago, if you'd spent an evening in a pub or restaurant the chances are that you'd have gone home reeking of cigarette smoke. Not any more though. The ban on smoking in public places that came into force in July 2007 means that you can return home smelling as fresh as when you left. More recently, another attempt has been made to shape people's behaviour through the introduction of a minimum price for alcohol aimed at curbing binge drinking and its attendant consequences. Such measures are aimed at certain sectors of society, but we're all increasingly challenged to think about ways in which we might need to change: to take more exercise, perhaps; to eat healthily; to adopt a sustainable lifestyle; to invest or shop ethically; and so we could continue.

We may think of all this as something new but, of course, it's not. Every age has seen its calls to reform, none more powerful than that of John the Baptist. His call to repentance boiled down to a simple challenge: are you ready to change? Responding to Christ, he declared, entails a radical overhaul of who and what we are, a turning from our old way of life to a new. And that's not just a one-off response. It's one we need to go on making day after day, for though we seek to walk his way, repeatedly we fail; though we strive to be different, so often we stay the same. John calls us, as he called his listeners centuries ago, to ask what still needs changing in our lives, to recognise and acknowledge our faults, and with God's help to seek new beginnings in Christ.

Prayer

Gracious God,
    show me where I need to change,
    where my faith is lacking and my discipleship weak,
    and help me each day to move a little further from what I've been
    to what you would have me be.
Direct my steps
    and put a new heart and a right spirit within me,
    so that my life may truly bear fruit worthy of repentance.
Amen.

14
Luke 1:11-15a, 18-20

Believing the impossible

An angel of the Lord appeared to Zechariah, standing on the right-hand side of the altar of incense. On seeing him, Zechariah was awestruck and paralysed by fear, but the angel said to him, 'Don't be frightened, Zechariah, for your plea has been heard. Your wife Elizabeth will bear you a son, and you are to call him John. He will bring you joy and gladness, and many will rejoice at his birth, for he will be great in the eyes of the Lord.' Zechariah said to the angel, 'How can I know this is true? For I am an old man, and my wife also is getting on in years.' The angel replied, 'I am Gabriel. I stand in God's presence, and he has sent me to tell you this good news, but now, since you have not believed my words that in due course will be fulfilled, you will be struck dumb, rendered mute until the day these things happen.'

Reflection

'Impossible! It can't be done!' That was the response of Zechariah to the news that his wife Elizabeth was to give birth to a son. Whether she was beyond childbearing years is not clear, but there is no doubt that any hopes the couple might have had of her conceiving were long since gone. They were reconciled to their disappointment, so to be told that a child was to be born to them after all must have seemed too good to be true. From a human point of view, it was a perfectly understandable response, but here we are talking about God. That is what Zechariah failed to account for, and that is what made all the difference, for with God all things are possible.

Do we believe that? There will be times when we find God's promises hard to accept; times when we look at our life or the life of the world, and we feel that both are beyond redemption.

Humanly speaking, that again is perfectly understandable, but once more we fail to account for God – the God who lived and died among us in Christ, raising him from the tomb; the God who has repeatedly shown that nothing is beyond him, however much it may seem beyond us!

Prayer

Loving God,
> remind me of the ways you have overturned human expectations throughout history,
> time and again demonstrating that all things are possible for those who love you.

Teach me, then, to look beyond the obvious and immediate,
> and to live in the light of your sovereign grace,
> which is able to do far more than I can ever ask or imagine,
> through Christ my Lord.

Amen.

15
Luke 1:16, 17

Preparing the way

'He will turn many of the people of Israel to the Lord their God, and he will go out in the spirit and power of Elijah, to turn the hearts of parents to their children, and those who have gone astray to the wisdom of the righteous; to make ready a people prepared for the Lord.'

Reflection

Go to watch any star or celebrity in concert, and, almost certainly, they will have a supporting cast. Turn to the first two chapters of the Gospel of Luke, and you will find something rather similar. The chapters are concerned primarily with the birth of Jesus, but there's another birth entwined with his, another character who figures prominently in his story, and that, of course, is John the Baptist. In fact, John is given a mention in the early chapters of all four Gospels, so, clearly, his role was important, but what exactly was that role and what can we learn from it?

The answer is very simple, and it's there in those words from Luke, chapter 1: 'to make ready a people prepared for the Lord'. This was John's task: to prepare the way of Christ; not in the sense of being a warm-up act, but rather as one who would get people ready to welcome Jesus when he came. For John that was to mean speaking out concerning the kingdom Christ would bring. It meant also following a distinctive lifestyle to reinforce his message. It meant pointing away from himself and towards Jesus. The lesson for today could hardly be clearer. We need to echo John's example in our own lives. Like him, we are called to prepare the way of Christ so that others today may meet him for themselves.

Prayer

Lord Jesus Christ,
    just as John the Baptist witnessed to you –
    preparing the way for your coming through his readiness to
    point away from himself
    and towards you,
    to live in such a way that everything he did,
    and everything he was,
    spoke unmistakably of the truth of his message –
    help me to prepare your way in turn,
    witnessing to your renewing power and transforming love,
    so that the hearts of many may be made ready to receive you,
    this and every day.
Amen.

16
Luke 1:67, 68

A time for worship

Zechariah, his father, was filled with the Holy Spirit, and uttered this prophecy: 'Hallowed be the Lord God of Israel, for he has looked on his people with kindness and redeemed them.'

Reflection

What words should you use to address the Queen, another member of the royal family, a Lord or Lady, or even the Archbishop of Canterbury? Do you know? I don't – and the chances are, if I were to be introduced to anyone so eminent, I would clam up completely, unsure quite how I ought to respond. We may well feel very much the same when it comes to approaching God. 'I want to respond to him,' you might say, 'but how?' To answer that in full would take many pages, but one thing stands out above all others in the Christmas stories, and that is the response of worship.

When Zechariah regained the power of speech, the first thing he did was to praise God. When Mary realised the full wonder of what God had done for her, she burst into joyful song. When the shepherds had been to the stable and seen the child in the manger, they returned, glorifying and praising God for everything they had heard and seen. When Simeon and Anna saw Mary and Joseph bringing Jesus into the temple, they immediately cried out in praise. When the magi reached the house where Jesus was, they fell down and worshipped him! For each one there could only be one response to the coming of Christ, one response that would do: to offer their worship in glad and joyful praise. Of course, there's more to our response than that, for worship leads on to service and witness in a wide variety of ways, but this is where it starts – in recognising what God has done, in joyfully acknowledging his greatness and in humbly offering our grateful worship.

Prayer

Sovereign God,
    like the choir of angels on the night of Jesus' birth,
        I sing in adoration.
Like the shepherds, returning from the manger,
    I give you praise for everything I have experienced of your love.
Like the magi, kneeling in wonder,
    I bring you my homage as a token of my love
    and a sign of my commitment.
All I think,
    all I do,
    all I say,
    all I am,
    I bring to you in reverent praise and joyful celebration.
Amen.

17
Luke 1:78, 79

The rising sun

The sun will rise over us from heaven, to shine on those sitting in darkness and in the shadow of death; to guide our feet into the way of peace.

Reflection

There's something wonderful about dawn, isn't there? It speaks of new beginnings, a fresh start – another day set before us, full of promise and opportunity. It is precisely ideas such as these that lie behind the wonderful words of Zechariah in Luke's Gospel; words that capture something of the wonder, joy and hope associated with the coming of Christ. Here was one who would bring joy where there was sorrow, hope where there was despair, love where there was hatred, and peace where there was division; not just a fresh chapter in history but also the possibility of a similar renewal in every human life that can only be compared to the rising of the sun; a new dawn!

That is what God offers to you and me today, to anyone and everyone willing to turn to Christ; a fresh start, a new day. And though darkness may sometimes seem to threaten once again, this sun will never set, but go on shining for all eternity.

Prayer

Loving God,
    teach me to walk in the light of your love day by day,
    so that each moment may be a new dawn,
    new beginning,
    rich in promise
    and filled by your love.
May the flame of faith burn brightly within me,
    so that something of your love may shine from me,
    bringing light and love to others.
Amen.

18
John 1:6-8

Pointing the way

A man named John was sent by God. He came to bear witness to the light, so that everyone might believe through him. He, personally, was not the light; rather he came to testify to it.

Reflection

It's funny, isn't it, how swiftly a little recognition can go to our head? A footballer scores a couple of goals and suddenly he sees himself as the next Wayne Rooney. A singer gets through the auditions for *The X Factor* and immediately starts to dream of becoming the biggest thing since Kylie Minogue. A contestant causes a stir on *Big Brother* and before you know it they're hyping themselves up as a national celebrity. We live in a culture which is all about 'me' – about thrusting ourselves forward, blowing our own trumpet, winning plaudits, making a name for ourselves.

Compare that with the example of John the Baptist. He *was* making a name for himself, undoubtedly. His preaching, teaching and ascetic lifestyle out in the wilderness were causing a stir, raising eyebrows among the religious authorities and attracting crowds in their droves. And as speculation grew as to who he could be, so his fame increased. It would have been easy for John simply to bask in the adulation, but he didn't. In fact, he did quite the opposite, pointing firmly and unequivocally away from himself and towards Jesus, the one whose way he was sent to prepare. That's what concerned him: witnessing to Christ and helping others to know him for themselves.

How about us? Do we share that same goal? Does anything we do or say point others to Jesus? Ask yourself, prayerfully and honestly: of what does your life speak – you or him?

Prayer

Remind me, Lord,
- that I am called to witness not to myself, the Bible or the Church, but to you:
- to what you said,
- what you have done
- and who you are.

Forgive me for losing sight of that
- and unconsciously putting across a different message;
- for confusing incidentals with what really matters.

Live in me,
- work through me,
- shine from me,
- so that who and what I am may prepare your way into the hearts and lives of others.

Amen.

19
1 Thessalonians 5:1-10

Be prepared

As for times and seasons, my friends, there is no need to write to you, for you are well aware that the day of the Lord will come upon you as a thief in the night. Just when people are saying, 'Relax, all is well', destruction will strike them as labour pains grip hold of a pregnant woman, and no one will escape. You, though, my friends, are not in the darkness such that the day should overtake you like a thief, for you are all children of light and of the day rather than of night and darkness. So, then, do not sleep like others, but be watchful and clear-headed. Those who sleep, do so in the hours of darkness just like those who get drunk, but since we are of the day let us remain clear-headed, putting on the breastplate of salvation through our Lord Jesus Christ, who died for us so that, whether we wake or sleep, we shall live together with him.

Reflection

'Be prepared!' Two words that all Scouts, past or present, will have indelibly printed on their minds. In theory, they should never be caught short, being ready instead to respond to every eventuality. But life, of course, has a habit of catching us on the hop, and although that can be a problem, it is also a blessing. Imagine how dull life would be if we could know everything that was going to happen and had exhausted its ability to offer new horizons and experiences.

It is not just life, however, that can surprise us but, above all, God. Take, for example, his coming to the world in Christ. For years, the people of Israel had looked forward to his coming, yet when the moment arrived many failed to see it. They thought they understood what God would do and were unprepared for anything else. The words of Paul to the Thessalonians suggest that *we* can do much the same. At first sight, they seem to be concerned simply with the return of Christ, but that is to miss the point, for Paul stresses that we do not know when that day will be, or what it will involve. We should live each day in a sense of expectation, recognising that God is at work in a host of ways, constantly able to surprise us. Do that and whenever Christ comes we will be ready to meet him. Strictly speaking, we can't be prepared for the unexpected, but we can be open to the possibility that God may speak to us and work through us in ways we have not even begun to imagine. Be prepared!

Prayer

Lord Jesus Christ,
> my expectations are small and limited,
> shaped by looking at life from a human rather than
> eternal perspective.

Forgive me,
> and help me to be prepared for everything you would do –
> in my life or the lives of other,
> today or tomorrow,
> here or anywhere.

Help me to live each day open to your will and guidance,
> and through welcoming you now,
> may I be all the more ready to welcome you when you
> come again.

Amen.

THIRD WEEK IN ADVENT

20

Isaiah 1:18

As white as snow

Come now, let us talk this through together, says the Lord: though your sins are like scarlet, they will be as white as snow; though they are red like crimson, they will become like wool.

Reflection

Are you the sort of person who dreams of a white Christmas? I am. Yes, I know snow can be a nuisance and a hazard, but I just can't help myself. There's something magical about the way a heavy snowfall transforms the world into a picture postcard scene, like something from a Christmas card or a fairy story. It doesn't last, of course. Before long, it's churned up into piles of slush and muddy footprints, but for a few moments all the greyness and ugliness of winter disappear.

For me, that idea is echoed in those unforgettable words of the prophet Isaiah. We all know that our lives are not what they could and should be, that there is so much which prevents us from being the people that God intended. Yet, says the prophet, with God's help things can change, not by our own efforts but through his grace. If we are ready to turn to him and admit our mistakes, he is ready to forgive and wipe the slate clean. No doubt, we will soon muddy the picture again, just as with that fresh fall of snow, but this time it is different, for the offer is always there to start again, however often we may fail.

Prayer

Gracious God,
    thank you that though I have no claim on your love
    and no right to expect forgiveness,
    constantly you reach out in love,
    eager to forgive and forget.
Thank you that your nature is always to have mercy,
    constantly putting the past behind me and helping me to start again.
Teach me each day to confess my sins
    and commit myself again to your service,
    so that I may receive the cleansing, renewal and forgiveness you alone can bring.
Amen.

21
Isaiah 46:9, 10, 11b

God's active word

I am God, and there is no other. I am God and there is none like me, pronouncing the end at the beginning and speaking at the dawn of time of things yet to be done, proclaiming, 'My will shall prevail, and I will fulfil my purpose. I have spoken, and I will make it happen; I have planned, and I will accomplish it.'

Reflection

Look at the label on any medicine and you will see there a list of active ingredients. Without them, your prescription would be useless, a mere placebo. There is a parallel here with the words of Isaiah, the prophet able to speak with conviction of the ultimate fulfilment of God's purpose because he knew that when God says he will do something he does it, his word being always active! There is never any question of him saying one thing and doing another, making a promise and then forgetting to honour it. He is wholly dependable, a God in whom we can put our trust.

That is the truth we celebrate at Advent and Christmas. These are seasons concerned with what God has done – not just what he promised but what he achieved! They speak of the God who has acted decisively in human history, wonderfully and unmistakably putting his words into practice! God didn't just wish the world well and then leave it to get on with its own affairs. He didn't just tell us what we need to do and then expect us to struggle on as best we can. He didn't give fine-sounding promises that remained only promises. He revealed love in action, the Word made flesh. That living Word continues to be active today, in our lives and in our world, and, through him, we know indeed that what God has pledged to do, he will accomplish!

Prayer

Sovereign God,
    thank you for being a God I can depend on,
    a God in whom I can put my trust.
Thank you for the assurance that I can live each moment
    with confidence,
    knowing that, though all else may fail,
    you will not;
    though heaven and earth may pass away,
    your words will endure for ever.
So I put my trust in you,
    secure in your love,
    confident in your eternal purpose
    and assured that your will shall be done.
Amen.

22
Isaiah 52:7, 8a
A time for rejoicing

How lovely on the mountains are the feet of the herald who proclaims peace, who brings good news, who announces deliverance and who says to Zion, 'Your God reigns!' Listen! Your watchers lift up their voices and together they sing for joy.

Reflection

Some years ago a prominent newsreader bemoaned the fact that only bad news seems to make the headlines. Sadly, nothing much seems to have changed; daily bulletins are still dominated by news of another riot, murder, disaster or tragedy somewhere in the world.

The seasons of Advent and Christmas, however, remind us of another kind of news, for the events they speak of were marked from the very start by a mood of rejoicing. When Mary and Elizabeth met for the first time since Mary became pregnant, Elizabeth exclaimed: 'The moment I heard you call in greeting, the child in my womb leapt for joy' (Luke 1:44), and Mary's response was to joyfully proclaim 'I rejoice with all my heart because of God my Saviour' (Luke 1:47). So it was to continue after the birth of Jesus, as angels appeared to shepherds with the message, 'See – I am bringing you good news of great joy that is for all people: today a Saviour has been born to you in the city of David, who is Christ, the Lord' (Luke 2:10b, 11). Finally, when the wise men at last reached their destination and entered the house where Mary and Joseph had taken lodging with their child, 'they were overwhelmed with joy' (Matthew 2:10). This is not to say that sorrow was at an end – the slaughter of children in and around Bethlehem ordered by Herod was to show this was far from the case. Yet, within the trouble and pain of the world, the tragedies and trials that beset us all, God had brought joy that nothing finally could overcome – good news that we continue to celebrate today.

Prayer

Gracious God,
> thank you for the joy you brought to Mary, shepherds and magi, as you entered the world in Christ;
> for the joy you have given to countless generations of believers across the centuries,
> and for the joy that you offer now to me.

Inspire me afresh with the good news of Christ –
> news of great joy for all people –
> and may I go on my way celebrating that truth each day.

Amen.

23
Matthew 1:1-6
Unlikely choices

Here is an account of the genealogy of Jesus the Messiah, the son of David, the son of Abraham. Abraham fathered Isaac, who fathered Jacob, who fathered Judah and his brothers, who fathered Perez and Zerah by Tamar. Perez fathered Hezron, who fathered Aram, who fathered Aminadab, who fathered Nahshon, who fathered Salmon, who fathered Boaz by Rahab. Boaz fathered Obed by Ruth, and Obed fathered Jesse who was the father of King David. David was the father of Solomon by the wife of Uriah.

Reflection

The opening chapter of Matthew's Gospel is surely one of the least inspiring in the Bible – or is it? At first sight, it looks like nothing more than a list of names, but appearances can be deceptive. Look deeper, and a different story emerges – for four of the names are anything but dull: Tamar, who conceived twins by her father-in-law Judah, through deceiving him about her identity; Rahab, the prostitute in Canaan who sheltered Joshua and his colleagues when they were spying out the Promised Land; Ruth, the Gentile from Moab who married Boaz and settled in Israel; and 'the wife of Uriah' – Bathsheba– who had an illicit affair with King David that led indirectly to the death of her husband. It was unusual in Jewish circles to mention women in a genealogy; more unusual still to mention Gentiles, and as for those like Rahab, Tamar and Bathsheba who had been caught up in tawdry sordid affairs – frankly, they'd have been seen as an embarrassment.

So what's going on here? The answer is simple and wonderful. Here is a graphic demonstration of God's grace in Christ, even before he was born. He came, not through the morally perfect or ritually clean, nor through the accepted and expected routes, but through those deemed imperfect, unsuitable and unworthy. The pattern was wonderfully continued in the choice of Mary, an insignificant girl in Nazareth; in the selection of rough-and-ready shepherds as the first to hear the good news; in the call of fishermen, a tax-collector and a zealot as his disciples; and in the willingness Jesus showed to mix with 'tax-collectors and sinners' throughout his ministry. Here is the God who has time for anyone, whoever that person may be; who has time for everyone, whatever they may have done. Here is the God who has time for you!

Prayer

Loving God,
> remind me that, for your coming into the world, you chose Mary,
> representative of the powerless;
> that to hear the good news first, you chose shepherds,
> representatives of the socially marginalised;
> that you called to follow you 'tax-collectors and sinners',
> representatives of the despised and hated;
> that you touched lepers and healed the diseased,
> representatives of the outcasts.

Help me, then, to turn to you,
> acknowledging my faults and weaknesses,
> everything that is wrong in my life,
> knowing that, despite it all,
> you have a place for me in your kingdom.

Amen.

24
Matthew 1:21, 22

Fulfilment in Christ

'She will bear a son, and you are to call him Jesus, for he will save his people from their sins.' All this took place so that what was spoken of the Lord by the prophet might be fulfilled.

Reflection

Read the Gospel accounts of the life, death and resurrection of Jesus and one thing will leap out at you: the constant references to events taking place in order to fulfil the Scriptures. In the opening four chapters of Matthew alone there are four instances, and so it continues through the remainder. Prophecies of old are seen to point beyond their original context to the ministry of Christ, finding there a deeper relevance.

Is this what we mean by the fulfilment of God's word? In part, yes, but Jesus saw himself as far more than the realisation of ancient promises. He came, he said, to fulfil not only the words of the prophets but the law also, that which lay at the heart of his people's faith. Everything this had attempted to do, he said – putting us right with God, bridging the gap that keeps us apart – was accomplished through him. The law prescribed outward observance; he brought inner change. The law called for sacrifice; he made that sacrifice once and for all. The law consisted of various commandments; he summed them up in a single command: to love one another. In him we see fulfilled not simply the occasional prophecy but God's entire purpose, his will for all. No wonder, then, that *we* are able to find fulfilment through him in turn.

Prayer

Eternal God,
> thank you for the way your word has spoken and continues to speak today,
> the way your message of old can constantly be reapplied to new people and situations
> and speak afresh of your love for all.

Thank you that the hopes and aspirations of old were realised in Christ,
> not only fulfilled but bringing fulfilment to all who put their trust in him.

Help me each day to grasp that truth afresh for myself,
> to find in him the one who makes sense of the Scriptures
> and of life itself.

Amen.

25
Matthew 2:5b

God's living word

For, as it is written . . .

Reflection

'As it is written' – those words run like a thread throughout the Gospel of Matthew and, indeed, throughout much of the New Testament, the message of the law and the prophets being seen as fulfilled in the birth, life, death and resurrection of Christ. So what is being said here? On one level, it reinforces the idea of God's word always being active, never exhausted until it has fulfilled its purpose. There is, though, a second truth that can be drawn from these words, which takes those observations a little further, for the fascinating fact is that the Scriptures cited as being fulfilled were, more often than not, initially addressed to a very different situation in an altogether different time. Suddenly, though, with the coming of Christ, they took on new meaning; imbued with fresh power and fulfilled in a yet more wonderful way. God's word of old was speaking again to a new time and situation.

Countless generations across the years can testify to that same truth in their own lives, words of Scripture initially concerned with events and people long past having leapt out of the page as though God were speaking directly to them. Here is the wonder of the Bible: that words so very old can seem so startlingly new. That is why we call it God's word, for, difficult though it may be sometimes to understand – occasionally dry, often complex, frequently mystifying – God nonetheless can speak through it today to you, to me, to everyone.

Prayer

Living God,
> break through the stranglehold of familiarity and complacency,
> and open my heart to your word,
> so that it may speak afresh to my life.

Teach me to read the Scriptures as Matthew read them,
> not as some record of past events
> but as a message that goes on being realised in new ways today,
> both in my life and the lives of others.

Amen.

26
Matthew 6:10

Thy kingdom come

'May your kingdom come and your will be done, here on earth as it is in heaven.'

Reflection

Across the country during the month of December, a host of children will eagerly be opening the appropriate window on their Advent calendars and counting off another day to Christmas. For many, young and old alike, that's all Advent is: a sort of prelude leading up to the big day. But, of course, it's intended to denote far more than that, calling us to prepare not simply for our celebration of Christ's coming long ago but also for the day when he will come again to establish his kingdom. Advent reminds us that, though we do not know when that will be, the time is drawing closer and will finally dawn. What then, it asks us, are we doing with the years in between?

'Your kingdom come', we pray, *'on earth as it is in heaven'*. That's the all-important detail. We're not called simply to sit back and wait for God to get on with it. Nor are we to regard his kingdom as being beyond this world, reserved for another place and time. The kingdom of God, said Jesus, dawned with his birth in Bethlehem and has been growing ever since; imperceptibly perhaps, like a seed slowly germinating, but growing nonetheless. And to grow further it needs us to play our part in its cultivation. Every deed of love we offer, every act of service, extension of forgiveness, gesture of compassion or expression of faith, contributes to the fulfilment of God's purpose. They may not seem much in themselves, but he is able to take and use them in ways that exceed our expectations. One thing is certain: if we want to see change, we have to contribute to making it happen. To pray

'Your kingdom come' means committing ourselves to building it now. It means asking not when it will finally dawn but what we are doing personally to help bring it closer here, today, on earth.

Prayer

Almighty God,
> remind me that true discipleship involves not just proclaiming your kingdom
> but helping to build it,
>> working in whatever way possible to accomplish your will here and now.

Give me, then, a vision not just of the future
> but also of the present.

Show me what you would have me do
> and help me to do it,
>> so that when I pray 'Your kingdom come',
>> I may truly mean it.

Amen.

27
Luke 4:18, 19

A time to give

'The spirit of the Lord has anointed me to proclaim good news to the poor. He has sent me to announce release to all who are imprisoned, sight to the blind and liberty to the oppressed; to make known the time of God's blessing.'

Reflection

If you listen out around this time of year you can't help but hear a jingling sound. No, not the bells of Santa's sleigh but the tinkle of money changing hands and of overworked tills as people across the country indulge in a frenetic spending spree. That's not necessarily a bad thing, of course. Shops and businesses depend upon healthy Christmas sales figures, as do countless jobs; and the presents bought, homes decorated, cards sent and festivities shared will bring real enjoyment to many. Yet how does all that fit in with the true spirit of Christmas? All too easily this becomes a time of self-indulgence, for frittering away money on what we neither need nor want and never mind the rest. Instead of being good news for all it becomes good news merely for us – a far cry from the gospel that Jesus proclaimed.

That's not to say we shouldn't treat ourselves to the odd festive luxury, but when you're buying that gift, that tree, those chocolates, those drinks, pause for a moment and think of what the money you're spending could do: the millions to whom it could offer help and hope. Think of the children it could feed, the people it could clothe and house, the countries it could help to supply with medicine and fresh water. For every pound you spend, why not give the same, or at least a proportion, to support causes such as those? The Band Aid song, 'Do they know it's Christmas?' puts things nicely: 'You ain't gotta feel guilt, just selfless; give a little help to the helpless . . . in our world of plenty we can spread a smile of joy. Throw your arms around the world at Christmastime.' Don't let this season simply be about giving to you and yours; make it a time for giving to all.

Prayer

Loving God,
    save me from turning this season of goodwill to *all*
    into one of good things for *me*,
    from indulging myself while a world goes hungry.
Help me to celebrate this season with my friends and loved ones,
    but also to think of those who have so much less than I do,
    those for whom the money I spend on little luxuries would
    represent a small fortune
    and could make such a difference to their lives.
Open not just my heart to them
    but also my hands,
    so that they, too, will have cause to rejoice in body as well as soul.
Amen.

28
1 Timothy 2:5, 6

Giving his all

Just as there is one God, so also there is one mediator between God and humankind, namely Jesus Christ, who – though human like us – offered his life to redeem us all, the message of this being proclaimed in the fullness of time.

Reflection

In churches and homes across the country at this time of year people will once again be lighting Advent candles. They've become a traditional part of Christmas preparations, a way, if nothing else, of counting down the days or weeks left until the big day finally arrives. For Christians, of course, they mean more than that, offering a simple but graphic reminder of what our festive celebrations are all about: the coming of light into the world. And, as many a sermon or family talk has noted, candles offer a particularly appropriate way of symbolising this, for not only do they shed light in the darkness but they have to give themselves up to do so. Each time the candle burns it surrenders a little more of its life until, finally, it is gone completely.

So it was with Jesus. Throughout his ministry he gave of himself, culminating in his giving everything as he hung on the cross. We cannot celebrate his birth without remembering also his death, his living without also his giving. He offered himself so that *we* might have life; he allowed his light to be snuffed out in order that it might shine in the darkness of this world and bring light to all. But that's where the parallels with Advent candles come to an end. When the latter are spent they shed light no longer, their lives are over and done with, but Jesus' surrendering of himself was not the end but a new beginning that opened the way to new beginnings for us in turn. The flame of his love continues to shine today and every day. Pause for a moment during this Advent season and consider what it cost to make that possible.

Prayer

Lord Jesus Christ,
    as I look forward to your coming and coming again,
    help me to remember the sacrifice at the heart of this season:
    your surrendering yourself for all.
Remind me that Advent speaks not only of your birth in a stable
    but also of your death on a cross,
    and that it is this alone that has made possible new birth for all.
You surrendered everything;
    gladly I offer my life back to you.
Amen.

FOURTH WEEK IN ADVENT

29

Isaiah 11:6-9

Vision for the future

The wolf will live side by side with the lamb, the leopard recline with the kid, the calf, lion and fatling lie down together, led by a young child. Cattle and bears will graze together, their young slumbering next to each other; and the lion will eat straw like the ox. Babies will play over the nest of a cobra, and toddlers will put their hands over those of an adder. Nothing will harm or kill anywhere on my holy mountain, for, just as the waters cover the sea, so will the earth be filled with the knowledge of the Lord.

Reflection

A vision of the future or sentimental nonsense? What do you make of these words of Isaiah? Are they poetic imagery or prophetic foresight? In terms of this life, at least, both those appraisals contain an element of truth. In recent years we have seen startling moves towards peace in some quarters of the world, yet there have also been unspeakable atrocities and mind-boggling inhumanity. Sadly, for every reason to hope there seems to be still more cause to despair, and, eventually, disillusionment sets in. We'd like to believe in a world such as the prophet paints – a new age of peace and harmony when violence, discord and hatred will be a thing of the past – but most of us take such claims with a strong pinch of salt. Life, we tell ourselves, is just not like that.

Such an attitude is understandable given the lamentable record of human history and the continuing divisions in our world today, yet it cannot finally be acceptable. *We* may abandon the world to its fate – God never will. He will not rest until his will is done and his kingdom established, on earth as it is in heaven. It may seem light years away from the world as we know it today, but we must never lose that vision of what life can become, nor stop working towards it.

Prayer

Gracious God,
    help me to recognise that my way of looking at the world
    is not the same as your way,
    and that where I see no prospect of change,
    you are able to transform situations beyond recognition.
Teach me never to lose sight of all you are able to do
    and all you are already doing.
Inspire me, therefore, to pray for and,
    in my own small way,
    to work towards a better world,
    through Jesus Christ my Lord.
Amen.

30
Micah 5:2–5a
From small beginnings

From you, Bethlehem of Ephrathah, small though you may be among the clans of Judah, shall emerge one who is to rule in Israel, whose roots go back into history, from the earliest of times. Therefore, he will give up his people only until the time when she who is in labour bears a child; then the remnant of his people will return to their kinsfolk in Israel. He will stand and feed his flock in the strength of the Lord, in the majesty of the name of the Lord his God. Thus, they will live in safety, for at that time his greatness will extend to the ends of the earth; and he will be the man of peace.

Reflection

'Every oak has been an acorn.' 'Small is the seed of every greatness.' 'Great weights hang on small wires.' 'Great engines turn on small pivots.' These are just some of the innumerable proverbs reminding us that unpromising beginnings need not be a barrier to success; and that, similarly, is a theme which runs throughout the Old Testament, from Moses taking on the might of Egypt to David killing Goliath, from Elijah triumphing over the prophets of Baal to Daniel facing up to the terrors of the lions' den.

The prophet Micah adds one more unforgettable picture to the list in the little town of Bethlehem. It is hard today to appreciate how extraordinary it must have seemed to hear God's promised Messiah associated with this insignificant town, notwithstanding its associations with King David. Jerusalem, surely, was the only place fitting for someone of such stature! In human terms, this may have been true, but not in God's. As so often before and since, God proves himself to be a God of the unexpected. In his kingdom the first invariably find themselves last, and the last first.

Prayer

Loving God,
    time and again you have overturned human expectations,
    using the most unlikely of people
    in yet more unlikely surroundings.
You have shown, beyond doubt,
    that no situation or person is outside the scope of your purpose –
    that all of us can be used by you.
Open my eyes, then, to everything you are able to do;
    to the way that from the most unpromising of material
    you are able to fashion the most astonishing of results.
Amen.

31
Luke 1:26-35
Who? Me!

Now in the sixth month the angel Gabriel was sent by God to a town in Galilee called Nazareth, to a virgin engaged to a man named Joseph, a member of the house of David. The virgin's name was Mary. Approaching her, he said, 'Greetings, you who have been highly favoured. The Lord is with you.' She was bewildered by his words, and contemplated what such a greeting might mean. The angel said to her, 'Don't be frightened, Mary, for you have found favour with God. You will conceive in your womb and bear a son, and you will give him the name "Jesus". He will be great, and will be called the Son of the Most High, and the Lord God will give him the throne of his ancestor David. He will reign over the house of Jacob for ever, and his kingdom will never end.' Mary said to the angel, 'How can this be, since I am a virgin?' The angel answered, 'The Holy Spirit will come upon you, and the power of the Most High will rest over you, so that the child you will bear will be called the Son of God, for with God nothing is impossible.'

Reflection

Surely God can't use me? How often have we echoed that response of Mary when God has asked something of us? The response is all the more vociferous when what God is asking involves sacrifice on our part. Yet if Mary's initial response is perfectly understandable, how then do we account for her compliance with God's wishes just a few moments afterwards? The answer is simple – she measured what was being asked of her not against her own resources but against God's. So it was that she offered acceptance – no doubt still confused, still wondering quite why she had been chosen, but ready to let God use her as he saw fit.

This story of Mary calls for a similar response from us today. We warm to accounts of the birth of Jesus, we celebrate his life and ministry, we give intellectual assent to the lordship of Christ, and we may be fascinated, even moved by it all, but God wants more. He wants us to be *changed*: our lives turned around, our very self re-created through his grace. He wants us to become part of his people and to use us in the work of his kingdom. 'Who, me?!' we may say – and that, of course, brings us back to where we started: to the quiet, trusting response of Mary to God's call. It is a response that resounds across the centuries, speaking loud and clear today: 'Yes, you!'

Prayer

Gracious God,
>grant me the humility I need to hear your voice,
>and the faith I need to respond.

Like Mary, may I be ready to answer when you call:
>'I am the Lord's servant.
>Let it be to me just as you say.'

Amen.

32
Luke 1:38

Ready to say yes

Mary responded, 'I am the Lord's servant. Let it be to me just as you say.'

Reflection

Imagine yourself, for a moment, in the situation of Mary two thousand years ago. You are engaged to be married and looking forward to your future, when suddenly you're told that you are to bear a child not of your fiancé Joseph but of God – a child who will change not just your life but that of the world itself. How would you have felt? And, more important, how would you have responded? Understandably, Mary was bemused. 'How can these things be?' she asked, and behind that question must have lain countless others. What would people say? What would *Joseph* say? Who was *she* to be singled out for such responsibility? Was she up to the job of parenting such a special child? Was she ready to have her life turned upside down, her plans thrown into confusion?

Many of us in Mary's shoes would have politely but firmly declined, coming up with one excuse after another as to why we were the wrong person for what God had in mind. But Mary was different. 'I am the Lord's servant,' she said. 'Let it be to me just as you say.' Had she answered differently, would God have refused to take no for an answer? Would he have pressurised her to accept his wishes, even continued with his plans regardless, forcing his will upon her? I don't think so, for that's not the way he works. He invites a response rather than demands obedience; he works through cooperation, not coercion. Mary could have said no, and God would have had to rethink his plans, turn to someone else. But she didn't. What God asked of her, she was willing to do; his wish was her command.

Less will be asked of us than of Mary, but God nonetheless needs our service and witness to help build his kingdom. He needs our faith, our love, our caring and sharing to help make him known. Each of us has a part to play, a contribution to make, but it's down to us whether we will take it on or shy away from the challenge. God will not twist our arm. Have we, like Mary, the necessary courage and commitment to say yes?

Prayer

Father God,
> thank you for inviting rather than compelling me to respond to your call,
> for seeking my help in working out your purpose
> rather than forcing me to submit to your will.

Save me, though, from using that as an excuse for doing nothing,
> for preferring my way to yours
> and resisting anything that challenges my comfortable lifestyle.

Show me what you would have me do,
> and help me to do it gladly.

Amen.

33
Luke 1:46-49

Magnifying the Lord

Then Mary said, 'My soul magnifies the Lord, and my spirit exults within me in God my Saviour, for he has looked on the lowliness of his servant. From now on and for all time, people will call me blessed, because the Mighty One has done great things for me. Holy is his name!'

Reflection

When I was a child I was given a magnifying glass; not just any old magnifying glass, but one so powerful that when I looked through it I could see things in enormous detail. I can still remember how it opened up a whole new world that I had never imagined existed before. A moss-covered wall near my home became a thick and lush jungle, and the tiny ant crawling through it became a terrifying monster rampaging through the undergrowth. Everywhere I looked, I saw things in a different light and on an altogether larger scale.

What, you may ask, has all that to do with the song of Mary? The clue is there in that opening line: 'My soul magnifies the Lord.' The expression is an old-fashioned one, so much so that many newer translations have altered it, but, in so doing, they have lost an important part of what it is saying. On one level, it is talking simply about God, but, on another, it is also about Mary and the way God had taken on a new significance in her life. Suddenly, a new world has opened up for her – a world in which she glimpsed God's greatness and goodness as never before, recognising that he was actively involved in her life and the lives of all. For Mary, of course, the circumstances were special, yet the coming of Christ, and his coming again to each of us through his Spirit, means that we too can taste that joy and experience a similar sense of wonder. Advent calls us, then, in turn, to catch sight of the awesomeness and sovereignty of God, so that we might thrill to his presence and join with Mary in declaring: 'My soul magnifies the Lord, and my spirit exults within me in God my Saviour.'

Prayer

Gracious God,
> open my eyes to the breadth of your love,
> the wonder of your mercy
> and the extent of your goodness,
> so that I may joyfully praise and worship you.

Give me a deeper sense of who and what you are,
> so that my life may speak of your greatness through word and deed.

Amen.

34
Luke 1:51-53

Beyond the margins

'He has displayed strength with his arm, scattering the proud with their airs and graces. He has caused the powerful to fall from their thrones, and has exalted the lowly. He has filled the hungry with many blessings, but has sent away the rich empty.'

Reflection

First class, second class or third class: those were the tickets available for the ill-fated maiden voyage of the *Titanic* on 15 April 1912, and they eloquently reflected the social status of those who bought them. In first class were the gentry, in second the well-to-do, and in third – or steerage – the poor, many having sold everything to buy their passage in the hope of escaping the class system and building a better life in the United States. The tragedy that subsequently unfolded was to throw all the passengers together, social divisions briefly forgotten amid the crisis, but in death they re-emerged, the bodies of first-class passengers being placed in coffins and brought back to shore while those of second- and third-class passengers were typically put in canvas bags and buried at sea. It calls to mind the notorious verse from 'All things bright and beautiful', long since excised from most hymn books:

> The rich man in his castle,
> the poor man at his gate,
> God made them, high or lowly,
> and ordered their estate.

Happily, the idea that some people are superior to others simply by dint of birth or wealth holds less sway today, but vestiges still remain, not least in the idea that a massive divide between the rich and poor is inevitable and acceptable. The events of the nativity challenge such a comfortable assumption. God chose to come into the world not through the affluent or powerful but through the poor, ordinary and looked-down-upon. He was born not in a palace but in a stable, not to an influential mother but to a young woman in the backwater of Nazareth. And the first to hear of his coming were not those at the top of the social tree but shepherds, representatives of those on the edge of society. In all this is a reminder – should any be needed – that the poor and marginalised matter to God. Do they matter also to us?

Prayer

Loving God,
> save me from turning my back on issues of social justice
> as though they are not my concern;
> from adopting an attitude of 'never mind the rest so long as
> I'm all right'.

Remind me that you came in Christ to bring good news to the poor
> and hope to the oppressed;
> that you care about people's welfare here and now
> and expect me to do the same.

Teach me, then, to work in whatever ways I can towards a better
> and fairer world.

Amen.

35
Luke 1:54, 55
Faithful to his promise

'He has honoured his promise to our forebears and come to his servant Israel's assistance. He has remembered to show mercy to Abraham and to all his descendants for ever!'

Reflection

'Ronseal', we're told, 'does what it says on the tin.' There's a clever reverse psychology in that advert, for the implication, though never explicitly stated, is that most products don't do what they're meant to – that their claims are bogus, their promises false. And that, sadly, is the way many people have come to view promises in general: to be taken with a generous pinch of salt. Pledges made by politicians prove to be spin rather than substance; guarantees and warranties turn out to be worth less than the paper they're written on. The fact is that, from earliest times, promises have been made only to be broken.

Perhaps that, more than anything, explains why so few people were ready to welcome Jesus when he came – simply because they'd given up expecting, their hopes in the promise of a Messiah having been dashed by years of disappointment. And yet come he did, the one anticipated for so long taking flesh and entering our world. As Mary put it in her song of celebration: 'He has honoured his promise to our forebears and come to his servant Israel's assistance.' Faith was not, after all, in vain: the waiting was over, the day had dawned, for in the child she carried not only was the Messiah to be born, but also everything God had pledged was to be realised, the truth of his word and faithfulness of his purpose finally vindicated. What God says he will do he *does* do – that is the triumphant message of Advent. It may take time, it may not be in our lifetime, but ultimately his promises will be honoured, his purpose fulfilled.

Prayer

Faithful God,
    thank you that in a world where promises are two a penny,
    made today and broken tomorrow;
    where so little can be relied on to deliver what it purports
    to offer;
    I can put my trust in your promises
    confident that they will be honoured.
Thank you for taking on our flesh, just as prophets had foretold;
    for bringing light into our darkness,
    forgiveness and new life,
    in fulfilment of your promises of old.
Teach me, then, to put my trust in you,
    confident that though all else may fail,
    you will not.
Amen.

36
Luke 1:67, 68a, 72-75

From fear to love

Afterwards his father, Zechariah, was filled with the Holy Spirit and uttered these prophetic words: 'Blessed be the Lord God of Israel . . . he has dealt mercifully as he pledged to our forebears and has honoured his holy covenant, the promise he made to our predecessor Abraham, granting that, having been saved from the clutches of our enemies, we might serve him without fear, and be made holy and righteous before him for the rest of our days.'

Reflection

Children, it used to be said, should be seen and not heard. Thankfully, that stern Victorian dictum is very much a thing of the past, but for many years it was rigorously applied. In the presence of adults, children were expected to speak only when spoken to and to do as they were told. Stepping out of line was typically met with a cuff round the ear or an impromptu thrashing. Unsurprisingly, fear was the result.

Certain strands of the Old Testament suggest that our relationship with God should be similar. Alongside descriptions of him as compassionate, merciful and slow to anger there are passages that portray him as harsh and cold, more likely to punish than pardon should we ever step out of line. And that's a picture of God that many still subconsciously hold. They see him as remote, aloof, an uncompromising judgemental God to be feared and approached with caution. Love rarely enters the frame. Yet, as the jubilant song of Zechariah above reminds us, any such picture was swept away with the coming of Christ. His birth ushered in a long-promised era and made possible a new relationship with God. No more trembling before God, no more approaching him with dread; love not only found a place but occupied the whole canvas, expressed in bold brushstrokes of trust, confidence, peace, gratitude and joy. That's the relationship God wants us to enjoy with him: one in which we worship him on high yet serve him without fear; in which, as his children, we are seen, heard and loved beyond measure.

Prayer

Almighty God,
> give me a proper sense of awe before you,
> of reverence, respect and humility as I worship you as the beginning and end of all,
> the creator of the ends of the earth and giver of life.

But help me to remember also that you took flesh,
> coming into the world through Christ
> and identifying yourself with humankind,
> and that you did so not to condemn and punish
> but to express the immensity of your love.

Whatever else I fear, then,
> teach me never to fear *you*,
> but to rest secure in your unfailing love, goodness and mercy.

Amen.

37
John 1:1-3a

The start of it all

At the start of it all was the Word, the Word being God as well as being *with* God. He was there from the start with God, all things coming into existence through him, and nothing existing without him.

Reflection

There is something unusual about the Gospel of John. Unlike Matthew and Luke, John does not start with Mary or Joseph, nor does he refer to Bethlehem, a stable or a manger; in fact, there is no mention of a Christmas story at all. Unlike Mark, he does not start with the ministry of Jesus either, though he soon moves on to this. He takes us instead to the dawn of time and the events of creation, as he reminds us of God's sovereign will there at the beginning of it all. Despite everything that would frustrate him and deny his love, he tells us, God's gracious purpose was active from the start, the living Word later to be embodied in the Word made flesh.

For John, the coming of Christ is not God's attempt to make up for a ghastly mistake; it is the natural expression of a love constantly at work, revealed in history, declared through prophets, and finally lived out in flesh and blood. John's testimony calls us to reflect on all God has yet to do in the light of everything he has already done.

Prayer

Gracious God,
> teach me that your loving purpose goes back to the beginning of time,
> and will endure to the end . . .
> and beyond . . .
> your nature always being to have mercy,
> to forgive, renew and restore.

Help me to appreciate the enormity of your faithfulness,
> and to use this season of Advent to open my heart more fully to your grace.

Amen.

38
John 1:10, 11
The forgotten person?

He was in the world, and though the world was made through him, the world did not recognise him. He came to that which was his own, but his own did not receive him.

Reflection

Have you finished writing and posting your Christmas cards? You may think you have, but, even when you've posted the last one, you can just about guarantee an unexpected card will arrive from someone you've completely forgotten about. Embarrassing, isn't it!

That person, though, may not be the only one you forget about, for there's someone else we all too often overlook, and that, astonishingly, is Jesus himself! We may sing about him, read about him and hear about him time and again, yet fail actually to stop and meet him. We can be so busy with our festivities, even our carol services and celebrations, that we miss out on the personal encounter that Christmas offers. Instead of offering a welcome, we keep the doors of our lives firmly barred. Instead of going in heart and mind to Bethlehem, we stay wrapped up in our own little world. Instead of receiving the greatest gift ever offered to humankind, we find ourselves asking why it hasn't quite felt like Christmas. Don't let that happen to you. Whatever else, don't forget the one who Christmas is ultimately all about and don't forget to respond to him.

Prayer

Loving God,
    in all the bustle of this season,
    I so easily forget what matters most:
    responding to the gift of your Son.
Forgive me for so easily relegating Jesus to the periphery of my celebrations
    rather than placing him at the centre, where he belongs;
    for doing so much to prepare for Christmas on the surface
    yet so little to make myself ready within.
Open my heart to welcome the living Christ into my life,
    so that I may rejoice in his love, not just at Christmas,
    but always.
Amen.

39
John 3:16
The God who believes in us!

'God loved the world so deeply that he surrendered his only Son, so that, instead of perishing, all those who believe in him may have eternal life.'

Reflection

'I believe in God, the Father almighty, maker of heaven and earth'. So say the opening words of the Apostle's Creed, a statement of faith designed to encapsulate the essential convictions of Christian belief; to summarise what we believe, or, at least, what we are meant to believe. Yet, all such creeds leave one thing out; a statement that, for me, is more important than any other, and that is the affirmation that God believes in us! We are talking, of course, about a different kind of belief, though it is not as different as you might at first think. What we see in the birth of Jesus is God firmly and resoundingly declaring: 'I believe in humankind!'

To understand the full wonder behind that statement we need to remind ourselves what, in the biblical sense, it means to say, 'I believe'. It doesn't mean accepting the existence of something, in the sense that we might believe in ghosts or flying saucers. It means belief in the sense of trust, putting one's faith in something, and being ready, if necessary, to stake one's name and reputation on the object of one's belief. Seen in that light, how many people do we truly believe in? Yet, that is the belief God has in us. He doesn't see us through rose-coloured spectacles. He is not blind for a moment to our fallibility and sinfulness. Yet, despite all that is wrong in our lives, he sees something precious in us, special and worth saving – even worth dying for! In the stable in Bethlehem, the child in a manger, and the life, death and resurrection that followed, we see God's emphatic 'yes' to humankind, his affirmation of our worth! The creeds are important, don't get me wrong, but they don't quite say everything, for it seems to me that if we haven't understood that God believes in us, we haven't really understood what it means to say, 'I believe in God'.

Prayer

Living God,
 when I look at my life,
 I see so much that is wrong
 and so little that is right.
I see selfishness, greed, envy and bitterness,
 rather than the fruits of the Spirit I so much long to show.
I see narrowness of mind,
 weakness of faith
 and feebleness of commitment
 rather than the vision, trust and dedication you expect from me.
I want to live and work for you,
 yet I seem incapable of doing so,
 and I despair of ever changing.
Help me to remember that you can achieve what I can never achieve by myself;
that *you* believe in me, even when *I* don't.
Amen.

40
John 12:46

The God who comes to us

I have come to bring light into the world, so that everyone who believes in me will not remain in darkness.

Reflection

There was a time when, should you feel too unwell to get to your local surgery, a doctor would come and see you. Not any more, or at least not as was once the case. There are some circumstances, of course, when a doctor will still come but the usual procedure out of hours is to get yourself to a duty doctor who will deal with your problem. The onus is on the patient to *go* because, quite simply, there aren't enough doctors to *come*.

We can tend to think of God in a similar sort of way – as one we have to *go to*, with the responsibility on us to make the first approach. Look, though, at the nativity stories in Matthew and Luke, or the opening verses of John's Gospel, and a very different picture emerges. Running through them all, like a common thread, is the message that it is God who first comes to us. He came to Zechariah, then Mary, then Joseph, and then to the shepherds out in the fields – the approach always at his initiative. He came bringing his word of promise, challenge, joy and hope, offering his love and his gift of new life – and so he continues to come today. Before we yet know him, before sometimes we even know our need, he draws near, reaching out in welcome, extending his grace. Yes, Christmas calls for a response, but it is not finally about us coming to God; it is, above all, about him coming to us.

Prayer

Lord Jesus Christ,
    come afresh into my life,
    and break through all the barriers I inadvertently set up against you,
    so that I may know you more nearly by my side
    and draw closer to you each day.
Speak your word,
    grant your guidance,
    and fill me with your love,
    so that I may go for you, who came for me.
Amen.

41
Galatians 4:4, 5
The fullness of time

In the fullness of time, God sent his own Son, born of a woman and born under the law, so that we who were subjects of the law might be redeemed, and, through adoption, become his children.

Reflection

Some people claim that there could have been no more opportune moment for the coming of Jesus than the time God actually chose. The Roman empire, they argue, brought unparalleled peace and stability, an opportunity to travel as never before, and an intermingling of cultures that brought an openness to new ideas – just the sort of world in which the gospel could quickly spread. It's a beguiling argument, but it doesn't work, for the fact is there are many other times in history for which an equally strong case could be made. If Jesus had come today, for example, how much more of an impact might he have made? Using modern technology, he could have relayed his message around the world in seconds. Instead of preaching to small crowds on the hillside, he could have addressed whole nations live by satellite. Surely, if any era qualifies for the label 'the fullness of time', it should be the twenty-first century!

Yet God didn't choose this or any other date we might suggest – he chose that day in the reign of the Emperor Augustus when Mary and Joseph had gone to Bethlehem to be taxed. Why *then*? We cannot say, for we do not know the workings of God's mind. His timing is of his choosing, no one else's. There is a lesson here concerning not just the birth of Christ but the whole of life. We may wonder sometimes why our prayers are not answered as quickly as we would like. Equally, we may find that God is calling us to grasp the moment when we want to hang back, reluctant to commit ourselves. Advent reminds us that God's timetable and ours may not be the same, and it asks us if we are ready to put his timing first.

Prayer

Eternal God,
    ruler over space and time,
    before all, in all, and beyond all,
    teach me the secret of patience
    and of trust in your purpose.
Help me to recognise that what may seem the right time may
    sometimes be wrong,
    and what may seem the wrong time may sometimes be right.
Teach me to bring my concerns before you,
    to seek your guidance,
    and then to wait on your will.
Amen.

NEW YEAR'S DAY

42
Isaiah 9:2

Light of the world

The people who previously walked in darkness have witnessed a great light; light has shone on those who dwelt in a place of deep darkness.

Reflection

The days leading up to Christmas are ones I always approach with mixed feelings. On the one hand this is a time that brings the shortest days of the year, a time when the hours of darkness extend for their longest, but on the other it means that we are turning the corner and can start looking forward again to the evenings drawing out as we move first into spring and then into summer. No wonder the winter solstice found its way into the rituals of so many ancient religions, for at a time when life is literally at its darkest it offers the promise of new light, new life, new beginnings.

As Christians, we celebrate at this time of year light of a different sort: that which came into the world through Christ. The theme permeates numerous biblical texts associated with this season. 'A new dawn will come from heaven, and the sun will shine on those sitting in darkness and in the shadow of death' (Luke 1:78, 79a). 'Suddenly, an angel of the Lord appeared before them, and the Lord's glory shone round about them' (Luke 2:9a). 'The star that they had seen rise went ahead of them until it finally stopped over the place where the child was' (Matthew 2:9b). 'In him was life, and that life was the light of all. The light shines in the darkness, and the darkness could not overcome it' (John 1:4, 5). That's what we celebrate at Christmas: not lighter evenings to come but lighter lives *now*, light that goes on shining in life's darkest moments, even the shadowed valley of death. Whether it's spring, summer, autumn or winter, 25 June or 25 December, it makes no difference, for this is a light that illuminates our path today, tomorrow and every day.

Prayer

Lord Jesus Christ,
    shine into the darkness of this world,
    into its suffering and sorrow, evil and injustice.
Brighten the lives of those who wrestle with illness, pain
    and infirmity;
    those who mourn loved ones or face the prospect of their passing;
    those who are poor, homeless or hungry;
    those who are oppressed and exploited;
    those who are depressed, troubled or weary.
Shine into the hearts of those who do not know you,
    those who reject you, ignoring, rejecting or even opposing
    your way.
Illuminate my own path,
    opening my heart each day to the radiance of your love and
    blessing.
Come through your Spirit and shed your light upon all.
Amen.

43
Matthew 1:18-20

Ready and willing

Now the birth of Jesus the Messiah took place in this way. When his mother Mary had been engaged to Joseph, but before they lived together, she was found to be with child from the Holy Spirit. Her husband Joseph, being a righteous man and unwilling to expose her to public disgrace, planned to dismiss her quietly. But just when he had resolved to do this, an angel of the Lord appeared to him in a dream and said, 'Joseph, son of David, do not be afraid to take Mary as your wife, for the child conceived in her is from the Holy Spirit.'

Reflection

The words of Matthew, above, remind us of perhaps the most forgotten person in the Christmas story: Joseph. He features, of course, in nativity plays, Christmas cards, readings and carols, but it's Mary, the shepherds and the wise men who tend to steal the limelight, leaving poor old Joseph as some shadowy figure in the background. Yet his story, as much as anyone else's, has much to teach us – not least about having the faith and humility to accept God's will, however uncomfortable that might be.

Put yourself in Joseph's shoes and imagine the mixed emotions he must have wrestled with, the countless questions that must have been whirling through his mind. Had Mary been cheating on him? Could he ever trust her again? Did he still love her, despite everything? Could he somehow hush things up? What kind of fool did she take him for? But reflect also on his final response: 'he did as the Lord's angel had ordered, taking Mary as his wife, but he had no sexual relations with her until she gave birth to a son, whom he named Jesus' (Matthew 1:24b, 25). Despite his misgivings he was ready to do what he believed God was asking of him. Knowing full well what others would say, what a massive impact it would have on his life, he was nonetheless willing to put God first. Are you willing to do the same?

Prayer

Living God,
    when your call challenges and disturbs,
    too often I push it to one side,
    unwilling or afraid to listen.
Forgive my qualified commitment,
    my partial and half-hearted discipleship,
    and grant me courage to be open to your voice
    and to respond faithfully.
Teach me to put your will before mine,
    and to walk wherever you might lead.
Amen.

44
Matthew 1:21, 24, 25
Who? Them!

'She will bear a son, and you are to call him Jesus, for he will save his people from their sins.' After waking from his sleep, Joseph did as the angel of the Lord had instructed, taking Mary as his wife, but he had no sexual relations with her until she gave birth to a son; and he named him Jesus.

Reflection

If there's one thing harder than accepting that God can use *you*, it's accepting he can use someone else, especially when that 'someone' is close to you. We think we know all about them, and, almost certainly, their faults and weaknesses are clearer to us than to most people. Any suggestion that God has singled them out for a special purpose is often met with more than a raised eyebrow. When those faults are writ large, then it's all the harder to believe.

What must it have looked like then, to Joseph, when Mary broke the news that she was expecting, only to tell him in the next breath that the child she carried was not the result of some illicit liaison but had been conceived by the Holy Spirit? How would you have responded in his shoes? A little scepticism was perfectly understandable. Yet Joseph, like Mary, was willing to let God overturn his preconceptions; ready to accept that God should use this girl he thought he knew in the most remarkable of ways. The circumstances in this case were, admittedly, unique, but the principle holds nonetheless for us all. We need to be open to God working through those we might least expect him to; and, above all, through those we are so close to that we mistakenly imagine we know everything there is to know about them. It may be that it is time to think again!

Prayer

Living God,
> forgive me for imagining that I know all there is to know about people:
> for presuming to judge their abilities and qualities on the basis of what I understand about them;
> for questioning what you can do through them because I fail to see their true potential.

Teach me that you are able to use everyone in ways I have not even begun to consider.

Open my eyes, then, to what you are doing in those around me, and help me to recognise what you may be saying to me through them.

Amen.

45
Matthew 1:22, 23
Truly with us

All this took place to fulfil what the Lord had spoken through the prophet: 'Look, the virgin will conceive and bear a son, and they will call him Emmanuel, which means, "God is with us".'

Reflection

'They will call him Emmanuel, which means "God is with us"' – so we read in Matthew's Gospel of the promise given to Joseph by the angel in his dream. But what does that mean? In what way, through Christ, do we directly experience God's presence? It's easy to use such language, but is it anything more than jargon? How far, in other words, is it backed up in daily life?

If God is with us in Christ, then you'd have thought his disciples of all people would surely have recognised it. But no. Take a look at the four Gospels and you'll see that, although they walked and talked with him throughout his earthly ministry, they failed almost entirely to grasp the truth of who he was. He'd shown them what God is like, revealed his love, yet still they asked him, shortly before he died, 'Show us the Father.' It was only after Jesus' death and resurrection that they finally realised that in this amazing man they had encountered God himself. As John puts it at the start of his Gospel, 'we have seen his glory, the glory as of a father's only son, full of grace and truth'. The truth about Jesus, in other words, begins at Christmas, but it doesn't end there. It involves not just the manger and the stable but the cross and the empty tomb, his sharing not just our life but also our death in order that we might share in his resurrection. Only when we look at the whole picture rather than just a part will we fully understand the wonderful truth of those words to Joseph: that God has become one with us in Christ so that we might finally become one with him.

Prayer

Father God,
    thank you for taking on flesh in Christ –
    one with me
    yet also one with you.
Thank you for the assurance that nothing will ever be able to separate me from his love;
    that through his Spirit he is with me always,
    to the end of time.
Help me, each day, to glimpse you a little more clearly through him,
    until that day when I know you fully
    even as I am fully known.
Amen.

46
Luke 1:34, 35, 38
Life-changing power

Mary said to the angel, 'How can this be, since I am a virgin?' The angel answered, 'The Holy Spirit will come upon you, and the power of the Most High will rest over you, so that the child you will bear will be called the Son of God, for with God nothing is impossible.'

Reflection

A remote Scottish island recently experienced a quiet but dramatic revolution. For years most homes there had no central heating, fridge, washing machine, television or even electric lighting. Now, though, wind turbines have been erected on the island and, for the first time, every home has mains electricity. A ready source of power that previously residents could only have dreamt of has transformed their lives.

A not dissimilar idea underpins the message of the gospel, not least the story of Mary. How could somebody so ordinary feature so prominently in God's purpose? What made her so special? The answer, of course, lies with God. Certainly, he needed her acceptance of his call, her willingness to be used, but the power that transformed not just her life but the world itself came from him. 'The Holy Spirit will come upon you, and the power of the Most High will rest over you' – that's what made the difference! It was the same for the apostles at Pentecost. One moment they were fearful and confused; the next boldly proclaiming the good news of Christ. Why? Because once again God's power flowed through them. All at once they had a resource at their disposal unlike anything they'd known before. And so it can be for us, too. We may question whether God can do anything useful through us; we may even be convinced that he can't. But he *can*, being able to use us in ways beyond our imagining if only we open our hearts to him. Alone we can do little; with him we can do much. Never lose sight of that awesome truth, for it can transform your life!

Prayer

Almighty God,
    give me a vision of what you can do in my life;
    of what, by your power, you can achieve.
Instead of looking at my own meagre capabilities,
    may I focus on your limitless reserves,
    your ability to turn weakness into strength,
    doubt into faith,
    the ordinary into something special.
Whatever you would have me do,
    teach me to look not at the scale of the challenge
    but at the scope of your power,
    and, in that light, may I gladly respond.
Amen.

47
Luke 2:1-5

In heart and mind

It happened at that time that Caesar Augustus issued a decree that a census should be taken of the entire world. This was the first such census and occurred while Quirinius was governor of Syria. All, therefore, went to be registered, each to their appropriate town. Joseph, being of the house and family of David, went from the Galilean town of Nazareth to Judea, to the city of David called Bethlehem, to be registered with his fiancée Mary, who was expecting a child.

Reflection

Every Christmas Eve, as a boy, I would sit by the radio with my family and listen to the festival of nine lessons and carols. For us all, it marked the start of our festive celebrations, and words from the opening prayer of that service have stuck in my mind ever since, calling us 'in heart and mind to go even unto Bethlehem and see this thing which is come to pass, and with the magi adore the Child lying in his Mother's arms'. That's what we need to do if Christmas is to come alive for us each year, if it is to speak to us with the same force and freshness, if it is still going to be good news.

The very familiarity of the Christmas message means that it can go in one ear and out the other, becoming just another part of our yuletide festivities rather than what this day and season is all about. We need to picture ourselves in the fields with the shepherds, at the door of the innkeeper, at the stable in Bethlehem with Mary and Joseph, on the road with the magi, beside the manger with Jesus, entering in heart and mind into their experience. Do that and we will recognise afresh not just what it meant to them, but what it means to *us* today.

Prayer

Almighty God,
> like your servant Mary, I magnify your holy name,
> praising you for the gift of Christ
> and committing myself to your service.

Like the shepherds, I come to meet him,
> to celebrate the birth of the Saviour
> and respond personally to his coming.

Like the magi, I bow in homage,
> seeking to offer my worship,
> my gifts,
> my*self*.

Like your people across the centuries, I give thanks for this day,
> rejoicing that the familiar story I know and love so well still speaks to my heart;
> that the one who was born long ago continues to bring new life to birth.

Help me today truly to kneel in heart and mind before the manger
> and to marvel at your gift of Christ.

Amen.

48
Luke 2:6, 7
Making room

While they were there, she went into labour and gave birth to her first-born son. She swaddled him in strips of cloth, and laid him in a manger, because there was no room for them in the inn.

Reflection

Anyone who has ever commuted by train to London will know all about the problems of making room. Carriages are already full to overflowing as the train pulls into another station heaving with yet more people. Or you may have travelled to the coast on a bank-holiday weekend looking for somewhere to stay, only to see the same sign in every window: 'No Vacancies'. The situation must have been a little like that in Bethlehem on the night of Jesus' birth. People of the house and line of David had come from across Judea to be enrolled in the Roman census, cramming into every house, guest room and inn. We can scarcely imagine what Mary and Joseph must have gone through as they searched desperately for somewhere to stay overnight.

That experience, of course, was a symbol of things to come: Jesus found no room in the hearts of many throughout his ministry and continues to find no room in the hearts of many today. We may imagine that *we* are different; that we have opened the door of our lives and welcomed him in, but let's not be complacent about it. The truth is that most of us only half-open the door, at best. We allow Jesus access to certain areas of our life but keep other areas ring-fenced. We make room when it suits us, but at other times give him our divided attention if any at all. It is easy to fool ourselves that such a response will do, when, in reality, Jesus is knocking at the door, still asking to come in.

Prayer

Lord Jesus Christ,
    forgive me for shutting you out of so many areas of my life,
    for turning my back on you when I would rather not face
    your challenge.
Help me to make room for you,
    not just this Christmas but always;
    to give you not some token place in my heart,
    but a position at the very centre of my life.
Come now, and make your home within me,
    by your grace.
Amen.

49

Luke 2:8, 9

Ordinary people

There were shepherds in that area, living in the fields and keeping watch over their flock during the night. Suddenly, an angel of the Lord appeared to them, and the glory of the Lord shone around them, and they were overcome with terror.

Reflection

The stained-glass windows were magnificent. Each panel depicted scenes from the life of Jesus, beginning with the annunciation, his birth in the stable and the gathering of the shepherds around the manger. For me, though, one detail spoiled them completely: each of the characters had a halo around their head; not just the angels, though that was bad enough, nor simply Jesus, but Mary, Joseph, the innkeeper and each of the shepherds as they gazed down at the Christ-child. It turned what would have been a lifelike and hugely evocative picture into something altogether different: a depiction of the way religion is so often seen as divorced from reality, concerned instead with surreal saintly figures who have little in common with people like you and me. The gospel, it seems to say, is not for ordinary mortals but for a special breed set apart; not about life as we know it but about some ethereal existence in a world far removed from our own.

Of course, that couldn't be more wrong, for the nativity stories, the events of the gospel and indeed the accounts of the Bible as a whole are concerned throughout with ordinary people, flesh and blood just as we are. The shepherds out watching their flocks couldn't have been more ordinary or less pious; they were simply going about the business of their daily lives. Likewise with the apostles: each of them was plucked from obscurity to follow Jesus. These were no plaster saints living in an idealised utopia. The message of Christ, then as now, was for real people in real situations in the real world. His call, his challenge, his promises, his way, relate not just to others but equally to you!

Prayer

Loving God,
    thank you that faith is not reserved for the select few –
    the good, pious or holy –
    but is as much about me as anyone,
    with all my faults and foibles, doubts and fears.
Thank you that the gospel does not just concern the spiritual,
    matters relating to faith or religion,
    but relates equally to everyday life:
    to the person I am,
    the way that I live
    and my interactions with those around me and the wider world.
Thank you that you have broken down the divide between
    heaven and earth,
    the sacred and secular,
    the divine and human;
    that your love is for all
    and your call extends to everyone.
Teach me to consecrate each moment of daily life to you,
    knowing that, through Christ, you have consecrated it already.
Amen.

50
Luke 2:10, 11

Good news!

The angel said to them, 'There's nothing to be frightened of; for see – I am bringing you good news of great joy that is for all people: today a Saviour has been born to you in the city of David, who is Christ the Lord.'

Reflection

What sort of stories make it into the news? Just occasionally an inspiring event or heart-warming action may hit the headlines, but ninety-nine times out of a hundred the latest reports are dominated by doom and gloom: another conflict, another rise in unemployment, another political scandal, another grim set of economic figures, another famine, another natural disaster, and so on. We grow so used to bad news that we come to expect it, life being seen as intrinsically negative.

Compare that with the announcement of the birth of Jesus. It wasn't simply news; it was *good* news, the best there could be, glad tidings of great joy for all people! Why? Because ultimately it has changed everything for ever. Yes, bad news still continues, just as real and bleak as it has always been, frequently hard to bear and testing us to the limit, but it will not be allowed to have the final word. Light will replace darkness, love will conquer hatred, good will triumph over evil, life will defeat death. That's what the gospel is all about: not any demands that God puts upon us, still less warnings of judgement and punishment if we fail to toe the line, but the glorious message of his love in Christ from which nothing on earth or in heaven will ever be able to separate us. We have something to celebrate and something to share, good news to make known to all. However things may seem, never lose sight of that truth or forget to make it known.

Prayer

Living God,
> hear my prayer for those who are struggling to cope with bad news,
> those who are frightened and helpless
> or who have lost hope altogether.

Hear my prayer for those who are troubled by the *prospect* of bad news
> and who fret anxiously about the future.

Hear my prayer for all who have grown so accustomed to bad news
> that they struggle to believe in the future,
> their faith in life and in you having been shaken or broken altogether.

Make known again the *good* news of your love in Christ,
> and into our hurting world bring peace, strength, comfort, joy and trust –
> glad tidings for all.

Amen.

51
Luke 2:12-14

It is *you!*

'Let this be a sign to you: you will find a child swaddled in strips of cloth and lying in a manger.' All at once, there was with the angel rank on rank of other heavenly beings, praising God and saying, 'Glory to God in the highest heaven, and peace on earth among all on whom his favour rests!'

Reflection

Do you remember the advertising campaign, some years ago now, which preceded the launch of the National Lottery? It caused quite a controversy at the time: a giant hand hovering over the rooftops of a town before finally a finger reached down to single out one household as the lucky winner of the coveted jackpot, backed up by the words, 'It could be you!' The suggestion was that the hand of providence might one day select us to receive a fortune. Did you take the bait? Many have, and a number of people have become millionaires as a result, but by far the majority of participants will have spent a considerable amount of money with little if anything to show for it.

Contrast that with the events of Bethlehem that we are preparing once again to celebrate. Here was the promise not of money on earth but of riches in heaven; a prize not merely for this life but for all eternity – the greatest gift ever offered. Yet this was no lottery, dependent on the whim of fate. There was no question of it *could* be you if you happened to get lucky. The message of the angels, the evangelists and countless generations of faith since is quite simple: 'It *is* you!' The promise of God in Christ – his gift of new life with everything that means – is not reserved for the exclusive few, nor dependent on any quirk of chance. It is yours for the taking, waiting simply for you to claim it – for you, for me, for everyone!

Prayer

Gracious God,
    teach me that the glad tidings proclaimed at Bethlehem
    centuries ago
    is good news for me today, here and now.
Help me never to forget that wonderful truth;
    never to overlook the fact that you have come to me in Christ.
May that knowledge burn brightly in my heart;
    a constant source of joy and inspiration,
    whatever life may bring.
Amen.

52
Luke 2:15

Seeing for ourselves

> When the angels had departed and returned to heaven, the shepherds said to each other, 'Let us go, then, to Bethlehem and see this event that has taken place, which the Lord has made known to us.'

Reflection

I learnt something interesting recently. Apparently, many people claim that the artist, Picasso, was left-handed; to the extent that several websites dedicated to left-handedness cite him as a celebrated example of such. The fact is, though, that he was *right*-handed, as can be proven by an examination of the photographic and historical records. What was it, then, that caused so many people to think otherwise? The answer is that they took someone else's word as fact; assuming that what they were told had to be true. It's an understandable mistake, for we often have nothing but hearsay to go on, yet we need to be alert to the dangers, for ultimately there can be no substitute for first-hand experience. Until we have seen the truth of something for ourselves, either by witnessing it or testing its veracity, we cannot categorically say that we know something.

    That is just as true when it comes to knowing God. We need to learn from the example of the shepherds, who, when told the good news that the Saviour had been born, went to find out for themselves. 'Let us go, then, to Bethlehem,' they said, 'and see this event that has taken place, which the Lord has made known to us.' We may have been taught about faith as a child; we may have been brought up in a Christian home; we may have sat in church and shared in countless services; we may even know the Bible back to front – it makes no difference. What matters is that we have met with Christ; that we have put our faith in him and discovered in practice the truth of his words and the reality of his presence.

Don't let your faith rest on someone else's experience, on what others have told you about Christ – turn to him, open your life to his love, and let the gospel be true for you!

Prayer

Loving God,
    teach me to base my faith not simply on the testimony of others,
    but above all on my own experience of Christ.
Help me, then, to open my heart to him,
    and to welcome him into my life;
    to know the reality of his Spirit at work within me,
    and to accept the message of his love not just with my head
    but also with my heart.
Amen.

53
Luke 2:16

Something worth hurrying for

So they came with haste, and found Mary and Joseph, and the baby lying in a manger.

Reflection

If you were to be told in church on Sunday that a wealthy philanthropist was in the street outside handing out wads of cash, how much time would you waste after the service before you went to find out if it were true? The chances are that you'd be out of the church like a shot the moment the final hymn had ended – if not long before! Again, if you were out walking and spotted an excited cheering crowd ahead of you, rushing towards something, you'd probably quicken your pace, eager to see what was happening. Some things in life are worth hurrying for. So it was for the shepherds after hearing the news of the birth of Christ. It's only a small detail, but it's an important one: 'they came with haste'. Why? Because the news they'd heard was exciting, breathtaking, wonderful; news they and their people had been waiting so long to hear – almost too good to be true! There was no question of waiting until the next morning and then casually strolling down to Bethlehem after they'd knocked off work. This was news that had to be investigated at once, not something that could be postponed.

Do we, I wonder, still feel that sense of excitement at the Christmas message? Do we still marvel at what God has done for us in Christ? Do we still catch our breath in wonder at the miracle of the Saviour's birth – God made flesh? Do such things still capture our hearts and fire our imagination, not just at Christmas but also day after day and week after week? We may have responded; we may have discovered the truth for ourselves long ago – that doesn't matter: the message of Christmas is still one to get excited about!

Prayer

Gracious God,
    forgive me for becoming casual and complacent in my faith,
    failing to make time to nurture my relationship with you.
Speak to me again,
    meet me through the living Christ,
    and open my heart to the renewing touch of your Holy Spirit,
    so that I may again share the sense of urgency of the shepherds
    as they rushed to Bethlehem yearning to know more of your love –
    good news for them . . .
    and for all.
Amen.

54
Luke 2:17, 18
Something worth sharing

Having seen it, they shared everything they had been told concerning the child, and all those who heard them marvelled at what the shepherds said.

Reflection

If I were to say to you the words 'made for sharing', what word or words would you automatically insert before them to make, what at one time at least, was a well-known catchphrase? The chances are you would think of that old advertisement, 'Quality Street, made for sharing'. I, though, have something very different in mind: the word 'Christmas'. You will see some logic in that straightaway, for Christmas is traditionally a time for sharing cards, presents and good wishes. It is a time also when families come together and share in a way that may not be possible during the rest of the year. For Christians, it is also a time for sharing in worship: nativity, candlelight and carol services.

Yet, special and important though all those are, they miss one thing out; something that we see in the example of the shepherds. 'Having seen it, they shared everything they had been told concerning the child.' Think about that for a moment, and then ask how far it is reflected in your life. Having seen Jesus, their instinctive response was to want to share it – to tell others the good news, to make sure that they too heard about what God had done. This wasn't something to keep to themselves, an event staged solely for their own benefit. In the words of the angel, it was 'news of great joy for all people'. I've no doubt we will share much this Christmas, and hopefully what we give will bring those nearest and dearest to us great joy, but will we share the greatest gift of all? Will we communicate what we have experienced of God's gift in Christ? 'Christmas, made for sharing' – is that how you see it?

Prayer

Living God,
> just as the shepherds went on their way, sharing what they had seen and heard,
> so help me to share my experience of Christ in turn.

Help me to live each day with joy in my heart and wonder in my eyes
> as I make known the love you have shown me
> and the joy I have found in your grace.

Amen.

55
Luke 2:19
Digging deeper

Mary stored these things up in her heart, pondering what they might mean.

Reflection

There was a time, as many of you will know, when it was traditional to put small silver coins into a Christmas pudding mixture, the lucky finders being allowed to keep these as an extra treat. How many broken teeth ensued as a result is anyone's guess, but for children that little bonus must have added extra mystique to an already special seasonal dessert. You can imagine them, can't you, digging carefully into their portion, scouring each mouthful before swallowing in case they should miss out on their prize? Wolfing it down would no doubt have been replaced by methodological investigation.

With Christmas, too, it pays to go beyond a cursory encounter and to look more deeply into things. We can, of course, simply enjoy the externals – parties, decorations, food, get-togethers and the like – or we can delve further into what it's really all about. Why did Jesus come? What does he mean? What can we learn from the shepherds and the wise men, from Joseph and the innkeeper, from the events leading up to the manger and stable and those that followed? The more we look the more we'll discover, the full wonder of what God has done and continues to do becoming increasingly clear. Don't hurry through Christmas with barely a second thought. Pause, like Mary, and ponder what it all might mean.

Prayer

Gracious God,
    teach me amid the festivity and merriment of this season to
    delve deeper,
    learning from the example of Mary.
As I listen again to familiar readings and carols,
    and hear once more the story I know so well,
    help me to consider afresh what it all means:
    what you are saying through it not just to others
    but also to me.
Amen.

56
Luke 2:25-33a
Keeping faith

There was a man called Simeon in Jerusalem who was upright and devout, eagerly awaiting the consolation of Israel, and the Holy Spirit was with him. The Spirit had disclosed to him that he would not taste death before he had seen the Lord's Messiah. Led by the Spirit, Simeon entered the temple; and when Jesus' parents brought in their child to honour the customs of the Law, Simeon cradled him in his arms and praised God, saying, 'Master, now let your servant go in peace, according to your promise. With my own eyes I have seen the salvation you have prepared before all the world – a light that will reveal you to the Gentiles and bring glory to your people Israel.'

Reflection

It is not just our faith in ourselves that can take a knock as the years go by; it is our faith in God as well. As another natural catastrophe strikes, another country is plunged into violent conflict, another friend dies of cancer, or another person is raped, mugged or murdered, it is hard to reconcile the harsh realities of life with the picture of a loving and merciful Father. The fact that society as a whole generally dismisses any talk of God makes it all the harder to keep on believing, harder to withstand the drip-drip effect of scorn and scepticism or sheer disinterest.

Yet the example of Simeon, and of the prophetess Anna whose story follows his, urges us to keep trusting, confident that God is at work and that, in the fullness of time, his will shall be done. Both Simeon and Anna had the courage to stay true to their faith despite outward appearances. Have we?

Prayer

Loving God,
> it is hard sometimes to continue believing when so much denies my convictions,
> harder still when faith is ridiculed or rejected,
> and hardest of all when hopes are dashed and prayer seems unanswered.

Give me strength, despite adversity or disappointment,
> to stay true to you,
> trusting that your way will finally prevail.

Renew my faith,
> revive my hope,
> restore my trust
> and rekindle my vision,
> so that I may serve you in quiet confidence,
> this day and always.

Amen.

57
Luke 2:34, 35
A costly response

Simeon blessed them and said to Mary, Jesus' mother, 'This child is destined for the fall and rise of many in Israel, and will be a sign that many will speak against, revealing their inner thoughts – and a sword will pierce your own soul too.'

Reflection

How much will you be spending on Christmas this year? Probably a lot more than you might think. Not only will there be presents to buy, which themselves represent a sizeable expense, but there will also be the Christmas dinner, boxes of sweets and chocolates, perhaps a few bottles of wine, not to mention Christmas cards, a tree, decorations and all the other odds and ends that go to make up what we see as a traditional Christmas. There's no doubt about it, Christmas is becoming an increasingly costly time, to the point that some people pay into a Christmas kitty each week so as to spread the expense over a year.

There was, however, another cost involved in the very first Christmas, which perhaps we can sometimes overlook. We see it partly in the response of Mary to God's call; her willingness to surrender her body to God's will. That alone, alongside the joy and privilege, entailed making a sacrifice, for life from that moment was never to be the same again. Yet it went further than that, for just a few days after the birth of her son there were to come those words of Simeon warning of a sword that would pierce her soul; words that must have cast a lengthening shadow across her life as Jesus inexorably took the way that led to the cross. It was Mary's willingness to accept the cost of service, as well as the rewards, that made possible God's gift of life. How willing are we to accept the cost of discipleship, in turn?

Prayer

Gracious God,
>I forget sometimes that alongside the blessings of discipleship there is also cost –
>sacrifices that will be asked of me;
>demands upon my time, energy, gifts and money;
>responsibilities I will be asked to accept.

Help me to respond gladly to whatever you may ask,
>knowing that, however great the price may be,
>the rewards will be infinitely worth it.

Amen.

58
John 1:3b, 4
Something beautiful for him

What came into existence through him was life – life that gives light to all people.

Reflection

When I was a boy, part of the magic of Christmas was simply walking down a street and seeing a Christmas tree in the window of nearly every house, lights twinkling cheerfully in the gloom. Whether they are real or artificial, once suitably adorned, Christmas trees provide an arresting focal point and encapsulate the celebratory mood of this festive season.

For me, a Christmas tree also graphically illustrates the good news at the heart of it all: the changed lives made possible by the coming of God's light among us in Christ. Just as the tree is turned into something special by the addition of lights, tinsel, baubles and so forth, so we, too, can be transformed – redeemed, renewed, refashioned by his light shining within us. And this change is no mere outward decoration but a transformation deep within, a realigning of heart, mind and spirit from self to God, from our way to his. The process, though, is not a one-off but ongoing, and is dependent on our consecrating ourselves afresh to him each day so that he can work his miracle of grace within us. Fail to make time for him, lose sight of his love, forget to respond, and we prevent him from working as he would. Don't let that happen. Put Christ at the centre of your life, this Christmas and always, so that he can shape you into something beautiful for him.

Prayer

Loving God,
>thank you for the way you are able to change who and what I am;
>for working within me to fashion something pleasing to you.

Forgive whatever prevents me from being the person you would have me be,
>and grant that, by your grace, a little more of you may be seen in me,
>to your glory.

Amen.

59
John 1:10, 11
An unwanted gift?

He was in the world, and though the world was made through him, the world did not recognise him. He came to that which was his own, but his own did not receive him.

Reflection

How many Christmas presents this year will end up stuffed in the back of a drawer or cupboard, or donated to a charity shop? More than a fair few. In this season of goodwill we feel almost duty bound to indulge in a frantic spending spree, buying a little something for all kinds of people because it's just the done thing, and plenty more for family and friends in a bid to make this time special. It's all done with the best of intentions, but the result, sadly, is a mass of unwanted gifts. Many of our carefully chosen purchases are simply not needed.

The opening verses of John's Gospel speak of another unwanted gift – that of God's love in Christ – but the irony is that this is something we all need, whoever we may be. In him is the secret to life, the answer to our inner emptiness, the one who makes possible new beginnings for all, yet – just as it was when Jesus first came – many are not interested, and turn their backs on what God would have them receive. What of you? Have you accepted what he offers? And do you continue to make it yours?

Prayer

Gracious God,
    at this time of giving,
    help me to offer the worship, thanksgiving, service and witness
    that you alone deserve.
At this time of receiving,
    help me to open my heart to your gift of Christ,
    making his love and life my own.
At this time of joy,
    help me to celebrate the good news at its heart,
    the wonder of your coming in Christ,
    walking our earth and sharing our humanity.
At this time of sharing,
    help me to reach out to those whose hearts are heavy,
    crushed by hunger, poverty, sorrow and pain.
At this *special* time,
    open my life to your transforming power,
    your love that is able to make all things new.
Take what I am,
    and direct what I shall become.
Amen.

60
John 1:12, 13
RSVP

To all who received him, however, and believed in his name, he gave the right to become children of God; children born not of blood or any union of the flesh, nor of any human desire, but of God.

Reflection

RSVP – four letters through which we ask people to indicate their acceptance of an invitation or otherwise. It's a way of politely asking the recipient not to put the invitation away and forget about it, or to delay their reply until the very last minute, but to respond as soon as possible.

There is a sense in which we see something similar in the events of the birth of Christ, and indeed throughout his life and ministry. First, it was Mary, asked to respond to God's word pronounced by Gabriel, and her response was swift and unreserved: 'I am the Lord's servant. Let it be to me just as you say' (Luke 1:38). Next, it was Joseph, challenged to think again about breaking off his engagement, his response equally prompt: 'After waking from his sleep, Joseph did as the angel of the Lord had instructed, taking Mary as his wife' (Matthew 1:24). Then, it was the shepherds, told that a Saviour had been born to them in Bethlehem, and from them too there was no hesitation: 'They came with haste, and found Mary and Joseph, and with them the baby, lying in a manger' (Luke 2:16). Finally, there were the wise men, seeing the star in the east and immediately following it: 'They knelt down and paid him homage. Then, opening their treasure chests, they offered him gifts of gold, frankincense, and myrrh' (Matthew 2:11). The coming of Christ was an invitation to respond, and it is an invitation that God continues to extend today – to you, to me, to everyone. It's no good just receiving it and then putting it away;

no good thinking we can put off a decision until some other time, for God is asking you, as he asked so many all those years ago and as he has asked so many since: RSVP.

Prayer
Gracious God,
> teach me that I need to go on making my response to the good news of Christ;
> that it is not a one-off thing,
> once done and then forgotten,
> but an ongoing renewal of commitment,
> a consecrating of all I am and all I do to you.

So, once more, I bring you my worship,
> I offer you my service
> and I dedicate my life to you in his name.

Amen.

61
John 1:14

My word!

The Word became flesh, residing among us, and we perceived his glory, the glory as the Father's only Son, full of grace and truth.

Reflection

There are some books, aren't there, that we like to read more than once? I've just finished, for example, reading *Jamaica Inn* for the third time, having been inspired by staying the night in the hostelry of that name, courtesy of a last-minute booking. Of course, reading something again is never quite the same as coming to it fresh, not least because we inevitably remember something of the plot, but we can still get much out of it, often picking up things we missed the first time round.

With the Christmas message, and indeed the Bible as a whole, that's especially so. Yes, we've heard it all before. But whether it's the story of Moses and the burning bush, David and Goliath, Daniel in the lions' den, Jonah and the great fish, Zacchaeus climbing a tree, Saul on the road to Damascus, or Jesus lying in a manger, we will find if we look deeper that there is always more to discover and new insights to be teased out, as details that we'd overlooked before suddenly leap out at us from the page. Why? Because *this* story is not confined to the written word but concerns the Word made flesh. It speaks not simply of what happened once, but of what's happening now; not just of what God has done but of what he continues to do. The one who was born in Bethlehem can be born also in you. What was good news for some is good news for all. As John reminds us, the story of Jesus is special, for if we respond and receive, it is also *our* story.

Prayer

Loving God,
    save me from growing over-familiar with the message of your love,
    from losing my sense of wonder and gratitude at everything you have done in Christ.
May the good news of his birth,
    the glad tidings of his life and ministry,
    and the gospel of his death and resurrection
    speak afresh to me each day,
    moving me to joyful praise and heartfelt worship.
Amen.

62
Hebrews 1:1-3a; 2:1
A continuing response

In the distant past God spoke in various ways through the prophets to our ancestors, but latterly he has spoken to us through his Son, whom he chose to inherit all things and through whom he created the universe. Reflecting God's glory, he is the precise imprint of God himself, his mighty hand upholding all creation. So then, let us pay heed to what we have heard, so that we do not stray from it.

Reflection

'Will you still love me tomorrow?' So runs the haunting refrain of the 1960s' hit song by The Shirelles. It's a question that Jesus might equally pose in relation to Christmas, a time when, unlike any other, our churches will be full to bursting as people gather for candlelight carol services, midnight mass, nativity presentations and the like. For a short time, faith resurfaces and the message of the gospel strikes a chord with the general public. But how many will be in church the following week? How many will spare Jesus a thought the rest of the year? How many will see faith as a matter of commitment rather than occasional response? The answer, sadly, is precious few.

We, of course, will be among those few . . . or will we? We may profess the name of Christ and worship him week by week, but does the message of the gospel touch our lives in the way it once did? Is our faith as alive as the day we first pledged ourselves to his service? Do we still see discipleship in terms of an ongoing relationship, a continuing journey? Or has our commitment become more a matter of dutiful routine than joyful response?

Responding to Jesus is not a one-off affair, done once and then able to take care of itself. It's something we must go on doing, working at our relationship, building up our faith if it is to stay strong. We may have loved Christ yesterday. We may still love him today. But will we still love him tomorrow?

Prayer

Lord Jesus Christ,
>give me a similar devotion to you as you show towards me –
>a love that goes on burning fiercely within my heart,
>as strong in the years ahead as it is today or has ever been.

Draw me ever closer,
>so that I will still love you not only tomorrow
>but always.

Amen.

63
Hebrews 2:14a

One with us

So then, since those children entrusted to him share his flesh and blood, he became one with them, in order that, through his own death, he could destroy the one who holds the power of death.

Reflection

Despite its message of joy and celebration, Christmas is a time of mixed emotions, meaning different things for different people. For some it will indeed be a time of celebration, bringing family get-togethers, parties, the giving and sharing of presents, the laughter of children, feasting and merriment. For others, by contrast, it will bring pain. It may be the memory of a loved one who has recently died that hurts, or of an earlier bereavement around Christmas. It may be the recollection of bygone years before children grew up and left home to start a family of their own. It may be the burden of sickness, disability or terminal illness. Or it may be the continuing suffering of countless millions across the world facing the ever-present reality of poverty, homelessness, hunger and disease. Many will have little, if anything, to celebrate, in worldly terms. Christmas may be a time of joy, but not everyone will be rejoicing.

Yet it is precisely here that we glimpse the true wonder of the Christmas message, for at its heart is the proclamation that God became flesh, taking on our humanity. In other words, he understands what we are going through, whatever it might be. He doesn't just sympathise with our pain and sorrow; he empathises. He doesn't stand aloof from the daily round of life, for he has shared in it himself and is involved in our human situation. Christmas *is* a time of joy, but it is not just for the joyful; it *is* a time of celebration but it is not reserved for those who are celebrating.

It is a time of good news for all, whether they laugh now or weep, rejoice or despair. God has entered our world so that, in the fullness of time, we may enter his kingdom where all, indeed, will rejoice.

Prayer

Gracious God,
    teach me that you shared my humanity,
    from birth to death,
    so that I might share your eternity.
For the assurance this brings –
    the knowledge that you understand the worries, concerns,
    doubts and problems that confront me each day –
    receive my worship,
    in the name of Christ.
Amen.

NEW YEAR'S EVE

64
Psalm 89:1, 2
Great is his faithfulness

I will sing unceasingly of your unfailing love, O Lord; I will declare your faithfulness to all generations. Your constant love is unchanged from the beginning of time, and your faithfulness is as permanent as the heavens.

Reflection

It's a slightly strange experience, isn't it, to thumb through an old diary? It's like looking into a window of time that once represented the future but now concerns the past. Engagements, events, appointments, anniversaries and so forth that you once anticipated are now either memories or long since forgotten: twelve months of your life that together comprise another chapter in your continuing story. What is the plot that binds all those chapters together, that gives meaning and cohesion to every passing year? For the psalm writer the answer is simple: the faithfulness of God. Through all of life's ups and downs, he declares, one thing never changes: God's unfailing love, unchanged from the beginning of time, permanent as the heavens.

It's a wonderful testimony echoed in the much-loved words of the hymn-writer Thomas Chisholm:

> Great is Thy faithfulness, O God my Father,
> there is no shadow of turning with Thee;
> thou changest not, Thy compassions, they fail not.
> As Thou hast been Thou forever wilt be.

That's the confidence with which we say farewell to one year and prepare to step out into another. No one knows what it will bring – laughter or tears, health or sickness, triumph or disappointment. What we do know is that, whatever it brings, whatever we face, God will be with us in it, to the end of time and beyond.

Prayer

God of the past,
   thank you for the way you have worked throughout history,
   calling and leading your people,
   speaking your word and honouring your promises
   through Christ.
Thank you for your part in *my* history,
   for having guided, blessed, forgiven and encouraged me as I
   journey through life.
God of the present,
   thank you for being at work today,
   recognised or unrecognised,
   continuing to move in countless lives including my own,
   your presence a daily source of help and inspiration.
God of the future,
   thank you for all you have yet to do,
   for the assurance that each day you will go on working out
   your purpose
   until it is finally fulfilled.
For your great faithfulness,
   yesterday, today and tomorrow,
   receive my praise.
Amen.

65
John 20:30, 31
The message that speaks for itself

Jesus did many other signs before his disciples that have not been recorded here, but these things have been written so that you might believe Jesus is the Christ, the Son of God, and that, through believing, you might have life in his name.

Reflection

I worked out recently that during my time in the ministry I preached well over a thousand sermons. That statistic brought home to me how many millions of sermons must have been delivered over the years, thousands more being added to that number every week. Do any say anything new? I doubt it. More important, I doubt any set out to do so, for the goal of every preacher is, or should be, simply to proclaim the age-old message of the gospel. Certainly, each will attempt to bring home afresh the significance of that message for new generations, and this may well involve exploring different approaches and angles, but ultimately the heart of what any may say will have been said many times before. Sometimes a sermon will succeed in its aim – challenging, teaching, instructing, inspiring. At other times, it will leave its listeners cold, serving more to obscure than to illuminate.

No doubt, the same has been true of the reflections in this book, some having brought home the wonder of God's grace, others having left as many questions as answers. No one has a monopoly on truth, still less the ability to fathom the full riches of the gospel. Thankfully, Scripture's ability to speak does not depend on any human agency, however helpful this may be at times. It has spoken across the years to countless generations and continues to do the same today, still having the power to transform lives and win people to faith in Christ. My aim in this book – and in its companion volume, *Bible Gems* – is to provide an aid to reflection;

a focus for prayer based on the words of Scripture. It will only have succeeded in its purpose, however, if it has prompted the reader to delve further into the Bible so as to encounter the message that, thank God, is able to speak for itself!

Prayer

Gracious God,
>   thank you for your word, your guidance, across another year,
>   offering a lamp to walk by and a faith to live by.

Thank you for the way you have spoken to me,
>   stirring my imagination,
>   kindling and nurturing faith,
>   confronting and questioning,
>   yet also renewing and uplifting,
>   each day assuring me of your constant love and gracious purpose.

Help me, in the year ahead, to hold on to your word of life,
>   to reflect on the glad tidings,
>   to stay true to the good news of Jesus Christ,
>   to make time for the message that speaks for itself.

Amen.

NEW YEAR'S DAY

66
Psalm 90:1-4, 10, 12

Time's paces

Lord, you have been our home across the centuries. Before the mountains were formed and before you fashioned this world we live in, from eternity to eternity you are God. You return us to dust, saying, 'Back to what you once were, you mortals!' A thousand years are like a passing day in your sight, as short-lived as the night-watch. Our fleeting span is seventy years, perhaps eighty if we are strong; throughout they are filled with struggle and sorrow, here today and gone tomorrow. Teach us to make the most of our days and so to discover the secret of inner wisdom.

Reflection

There comes a time in our lives when it dawns on us that we are not as young as we used to be. Whereas the future once seemed to stretch out indefinitely, suddenly it appears all too short, the time left to fulfil our dreams being far less than we thought. Time and tide, as they say, waits for no one. It would be easy to move from here to a maudlin self-pity, but instead the psalmist turns to focus on God whose eternal nature stands in such contrast to our own transience. In the context of faith, the passage of time should not be seen as the years running out so much as life moving on, one more step along an unfolding journey in which there is always more to be discovered and new joys to be experienced.

Of course, we will sometimes remember the past with a tinge of regret, and look to the future with a degree of anxiety, but we should also recognise each day as God's gift, and live each one of them in the assurance that nothing will ever separate us from his love made known in Christ.

Prayer

Everlasting God,
    send me out into the coming year,
    confident that, whatever it may bring,
    you will be with me in it,
    and that your loving purpose will not fail.
Teach me to make the most of each day,
    living it to the full,
    and celebrating your great love that gives meaning to each moment of this life
    and the next.
Amen.

Ecclesiastes 11:7

The time of our life

How good and pleasing it is to see the light of each day. Celebrate every year of your life.

Reflection

How do you greet the thought of another year? Does it thrill you with a sense of new beginnings or does it bring an uneasy sense of time passing faster than you'd like it to? Hopefully it's the former, but on occasions over the coming months we'll probably all see time as a foe rather than a friend. When life is good, we want it to stand still so that we can hang on to it for ever – only, of course, we can't, and those special moments soon become distant memories. When life is busy, we want more time, for there simply isn't enough to go round. When life is dull, bringing yet more of the same old routine, time drags interminably. For a host of reasons we can end up yearning for extra time or wishing it away, and in each case we fail to appreciate the time we have.

How, then, do we escape from that impasse? Let me suggest three points to keep in mind. First, no matter what our responsibilities, we must learn to take things at a more leisurely pace, building into each day a few moments to be still in the presence of God. Second, we need to take things as they come, letting go of worries about the future or regrets concerning the past and remembering that each moment is God's gift. Third, we must remember that we live in the context not simply of our brief human span, but of God's eternity. In other words, quite literally, we have all the time in the world, and more! Yes, we'll still occasionally end up chasing our tails, wishing we could stop the clock or wondering why its hands seem to move so slowly, but we'll have also learnt to appreciate the time God has given and so to appreciate life to the full.

Prayer

Thank you, Lord, for a new day,
   new month,
   new year,
   waiting to unfold its secrets.
Thank you for the truth that, with you,
   not just *some* days are special,
   but *all* of them,
   each offering new experiences of your love
   and fresh opportunities to celebrate.
Teach me, then, as I celebrate this day,
   to celebrate *every* day,
   to see each moment as your gift to be gratefully received and joyfully lived,
   through Jesus Christ my Lord.
Amen.

EPIPHANY

68
Matthew 2:1, 2
Wise men still seek him

Following the birth of Jesus in Bethlehem of Judea during the reign of King Herod, magi arrived in Jerusalem from the east, saying, 'Where is the one born king of the Jews, for we saw his star rising in the east and have come to pay our respects.'

Reflection

There's a pithy little saying often still displayed around Christmas time on a church notice board, car windscreen or suchlike. The words? 'Wise men still seek him.' And, of course, that's perfectly true, for there are many today, just as there have always been, who still search in vain to find faith. It's not that they don't want to believe – quite the opposite – but there is so much in the world they cannot make sense of, so much that seems to contradict the God of love preached in the Christian faith. It would have been easy for the wise men to give up on their search, not least when they arrived in Bethlehem to find that no one had any idea who or what they were talking about. Could there have been some mistake? Had their journey been a waste of time? Yet they kept on searching and trusting until, finally, they came to the place where the child lay.

We, too, need the courage to keep on seeking throughout the course of our discipleship. If we persevere on the journey, searching for deeper understanding despite everything that appears to challenge God's purpose and obscure his love, we will find our questions answered and the confusion resolved as we glimpse for ourselves the wonder of God revealed in Christ. As Jesus himself urged his followers: 'Seek, and you will find . . . knock and the door will be opened to you.' The path in Christian discipleship may not always be clear to us; we walk by faith, not by sight, and much will remain hidden; but if we, like the magi, are wise, we too will keep on searching until we find what we seek.

Prayer

Lord Jesus Christ,
> as I look for answers to the mysteries of life and faith,
> there is so much that puzzles and perplexes.

The more I discover,
> the more I realise how little I have understood.

Give me the determination of the wise men to seek until I find,
> despite all that obscures you,
> until at last my perseverance is rewarded
> and I grasp the truth more fully.

Amen.

69
Matthew 2:3, 4

A mixed response

When King Herod heard this, he and all Jerusalem were anxious. So, summoning together all the chief priests and scribes of the nation, he asked them where the birth of the Messiah was foretold to take place.

Reflection

One person's meat, it's said, is another's poison. In other words, we react to things in very different ways. That truth is graphically illustrated in the journey of the magi, for we see there how, from the beginning, Jesus met with hugely contrasting responses: acceptance by some, rejection by others – a curious mixture of love and hatred, welcome and opposition that was to continue throughout his ministry.

Magi, on the one hand, set off on a journey into the unknown to meet the Christ-child. And when they found him, they knelt down and offered their gifts in joyful worship.

In stark contrast stands the figure of Herod, greeting the news of a new-born king with consternation and swiftly resolving to do away with him. For him, Jesus was a threat, a potential challenge to his authority, or so at least he imagined. His thirst for power and prestige closed his eyes to the fact that this child was as much good news for him as for anyone.

The pattern continues to this day, some being *for* Jesus, others *against*; some worshipping him as Lord, others being indifferent or hostile to his claims. Why the divergence? Who can say? The reasons are many and varied. We can no more account for why strangers from the East were irresistibly drawn to Jesus than for why those schooled in expecting the Messiah should have failed to recognise him when he came. But it's not what others think or do that matters. It's what *we* think, what *we* do, how *we* respond. What's your answer to that?

Prayer

Lord Jesus Christ,
 for my failure to welcome you as I should,
 my keeping you at arm's length,
 my resistance to your will,
 forgive me.
Overcome my disobedience, apathy and weakness,
 and help me to give you the place you deserve,
 at the centre of my life.
Amen.

70
Matthew 2:7, 8

A careful search

Herod secretly summoned the wise men and ascertained from them exactly when the star had appeared. Then he sent them to Bethlehem, saying, 'Go and search carefully for the child; and when you have found him, bring word to me, so that I, in turn, may go and offer homage.'

Reflection

Familiarity, it is said, breeds contempt, and if ever there is a danger of that it must surely be in relation to the Christmas message. We know the story so well – too well – having heard it so many times that we no longer take in sometimes what we are hearing. We listen to the words of Scripture and sing well-loved carols, but they wash over us, no longer firing our imagination as they once did.

It is worth reflecting occasionally on those words of Herod to the magi as he sent them off to Bethlehem. The situation, of course, is different, in that they were seeking someone they had not yet met, encountering Jesus for the first time, but his words are nonetheless just as appropriate for those of us today who have known and followed Jesus for as long as we can remember. 'Go and make a careful search for the child.' Do that, not just today but every day, and what we find may still surprise us.

Prayer

Lord Jesus Christ,
    teach me to search for a deeper knowledge of you
    as eagerly and whole-heartedly as the day I first knew you for myself.
Though the journey is long
    and the obstacles along the way are many,
    help me to strive to know you better,
    until that day when I enter your kingdom
    and meet you face to face.
Amen.

71
Matthew 2:9, 10
Never too late

After listening to the king, they set off again; and as they went the star that they'd seen rising went ahead of them until it came to rest above the place where the child lay. On seeing the star come to a halt, they were beside themselves with joy.

Reflection

When did the magi visit the Christ-child? They're typically portrayed as arriving shortly after the shepherds, but they almost certainly came considerably later, maybe over a year after Jesus' birth. How do we know this? Because they arrived not at a stable but at a house, and when Herod resolved to kill his new-born rival he ordered that all boys aged two and under should be put to the sword. In other words, a considerable time had elapsed from the time the magi saw the star to the completion of their journey, in no small part due to the delay they encountered in Jerusalem. We can only imagine the frustration they must have endured as the days passed with no end in sight, matched only by their joy and relief when they finally made it to their destination. Late perhaps, but better late than never.

We can learn much from their epic pilgrimage, not least that it's never too late to respond. We may have put off facing the challenge of Christ, not wanting to make a firm act of commitment despite being attracted by his message. We may have made that commitment but then lost our way, our faith being a shadow of what it once was. We may still be committed but feel we have failed in some way and that there's no way back for us. Or it may be that we're resisting some avenue of service to which God is calling us, hesitant as to what it may involve. Whatever it is and however long it may have been, it's never too late to put things right. Jesus is always ready to welcome us, eager to receive those who truly seek him. It may have taken you longer than it should to make your response, but don't let that stop you. It's not *when* you do, but *whether* you do that matters.

Prayer

Lord Jesus Christ,
    teach me that whatever I've failed to do,
    there is still time to do it;
    that however long I've left things,
    it is never too late to respond.
So then,
    whatever I have left undone,
    help me to do it now.
Amen.

72
Matthew 2:11b, 12
Which way now?

Then, opening their treasure chests, they offered him gifts of gold, frankincense, and myrrh. And having been warned in a dream not to return to Herod, they left for their own country by another road.

Reflection

I knew the route like the back of my hand, so I hadn't given the journey more than a moment's thought until we were confronted by a large sign declaring 'Road closed: diversion'. I should, of course, have simply followed the signs until we re-joined our intended route, but foolishly I decided I knew better. Only it wasn't that simple, and before long we were hopelessly lost. Much driving and a considerable time later we finally got tabs on our position – not far off, it turned out, from where we'd started! A salutary lesson, you might think, and perhaps it was, but on the plus side we explored parts of the countryside we'd never otherwise have visited, and subsequently, after consulting the map at length, we realised that there was indeed a short cut through that maze of lanes – a discovery that we were to exploit many times in following years on repeat journeys.

The magi, in a sense, were to come across a 'Road closed' sign, a dream causing them to return to their country by another route. Why? Because God had warned them not to return to Herod. But they returned via another route in another sense also. They'd knelt, remember, before a little child, presenting priceless and precious gifts, each of them clearly aware that they were privileged to share in a truly historic and special moment. Could they have just gone back home afterwards as though nothing had changed? Surely not. What they had seen and experienced must in some way have changed their lives for ever, for they had been touched by the divine.

So it is for us all. Truly to meet with Christ is a life-changing experience. We cannot simply nod in acknowledgement and continue blithely on our way. His love, grace and goodness call for a response, inviting us to journey in faith. Have we, like the magi, the courage to change direction and travel with him?

Prayer

Lord Jesus Christ,
    show me where you would have me go,
    what you would have me do,
    how you would have me live,
    and help me obediently to follow,
    trusting you to guide.
Amen.

WEEK OF PRAYER FOR CHRISTIAN UNITY

73
Psalm 133:1-3
Living in peace

How good and pleasant it is when kindred live together in unity! It is as fragrant as oil poured over the head and running down upon the beard, running down the beard of Aaron and over the collar of his robes. It is like the dew of Hermon falling on the mountains of Zion. There the Lord grants his blessing, life for all eternity.

Reflection

There are few things more sad, yet more common, than a family divided among itself. Yet it's something we see over and over again: husbands who no longer speak to wives; children who have fallen out with their parents; brothers, sisters, cousins, nephews, aunts and uncles, each disowning the other and refusing to have any further dealings with them. As if that isn't sad enough, invariably the cause of such bad feeling is something trivial, blown up out of all proportion over the years because of an unwillingness to meet and resolve the issue. Unchecked, the poison festers, feeding on itself and destroying the lives of all concerned.

Whether it was a dispute such as this that inspired Psalm 133, or whether it was something more complex, I do not know. The reminder this simple psalm gives of the importance of living together in harmony is, however, one we would all do well to consider, whether at the level of our immediate family or the family of the Church. The relationships we are intended to enjoy in both are special; we simply cannot afford to waste them.

Prayer
Lord of all,
    forgive the divisions that separate person from person,
    community from community,
    Christian from Christian,
    nation from nation.
Help me, so far as it lies with me, to live in harmony with all,
    and when that harmony is broken
    teach me to act as peacemaker,
    healing hurts,
    restoring trust
    and breaking down barriers,
    in the name of Christ,
    who will finally reconcile all things to himself.
Amen.

74
Luke 9:49, 50
One people?

'Master,' said John, 'we spotted somebody exorcising demons in your name, but because he wasn't one of us we ordered him to stop.' Then Jesus answered, 'Don't stop him; anyone who is not against you is for you.'

Reflection

When the Stockholm Conference was convened in 1925 to discuss the possibility of Christian unity, that objective seemed an impossible dream, an idea so revolutionary that most people shook their heads and predicted it could never happen. After all, the Church had been divided for centuries, often bitterly. Today, though, ecumenism barely occasions a raised eyebrow. We may not be one organic Church but, generally, members of each denomination not only respect those of others but are more than happy to work and worship together.

So is the Church more united than it used to be? Sadly not, for in place of old divisions new ones have arisen, often as entrenched and bitter as those that have gone before. They revolve today around issues of worship, church practice, gifts of the Spirit, women priests, gay clergy and the like, even – would you believe – creationism, and there are plenty on the basis of such issues willing not only to censure others but even to question and deny their faith. New orthodoxies have taken the place of the old. All of us would do well to heed the counsel of tolerance offered by Jesus to his disciples: 'Anyone who is not against you is for you' (Luke 9:50). In other words, you're on the same side. All right, so others may not see everything in exactly the same way that we do, but that doesn't give us the right to judge our brothers and sisters in Christ, to automatically assume that we're right and they're wrong. If we were all less keen to claim divine sanction for our personal convictions, however deeply held, what a difference it would make to our living and working together, and what an impact we could then potentially make.

Prayer

Lord Jesus Christ,
    help me to recognise that differences need not lead to division,
    that there is a place for healthy diversity within your body
    and that contrasting –
    even opposing –
    points of view can help stimulate fruitful and enriching dialogue.
Save me from writing off, as wrong, opinions other than my own
    and, above all, from writing off those who hold them.
Amen.

75
1 Corinthians 1:10
An unbreakable bond

I appeal to you, brothers and sisters, in the name of our Lord Jesus Christ, agree among yourselves and avoid any division, so that you may be perfectly joined, of the same mind and united in a common purpose.

Reflection

Have you ever tried sticking metal with wood glue, or plastic with wallpaper paste? If you have, then you'll know you were wasting your time, for you were using the wrong tool for the job. Different glues are designed for different tasks, and what works for one may not work for another. Get it right, however, and you will create a bond to last.

Such *should* be the effect of the love we are meant to share as Christians. The reality, sadly, is very different. For all the moves in recent years towards Church unity, there are as many if not more divisions today than ever, splinter groups continually breaking away over questions of doctrine, worship and church practice. Individual fellowships are equally marred by gossip, cliques, personality clashes, backbiting and so on. All too often, instead of testifying to the love of Christ, our relationship with other Christians speaks instead of our human fallibility, turning people away from the Church instead of drawing them towards it. There will always, of course, be differences of opinion and outlook among us, for we are all individuals with unique experiences of Christ. Similarly, there will be those we are more naturally drawn towards than others; that is a simple fact of life. If, though, we are truly 'in Christ', then the faith we share should transcend such differences, the love that unites us being more powerful than anything that may divide.

Prayer

Gracious God,
> for all my talk of love and fellowship,
> I am not very good at loving others,
> too easily allowing divisions and differences to sour my relationships.

For all my talk of being part of your family,
> I close my mind to so many brothers and sisters in Christ.

Forgive me,
> and open my mind to the unity of faith that I share with your people in every place.

Give me a concern for and openness to all.
Fill your Church with love,
> and bind us together,
> to the glory of your name.

Amen.

1 Corinthians 12:12, 15-20

Celebrating our diversity

Just as the body is a unit having many members, with all the members, though many, being part of the one body, so it is with the body of Christ. If the foot were to say, because I am not a hand I am not part of the body, would it be any less a part of the body? If the ear were to say, because I am not an eye, I am not part of the body, would it not be part of it? If the whole body were an eye, how would we hear? If all were given over to hearing, how would we smell? God, however, has arranged every part of the body as he wants it to be. If there were only one part, how could we talk of a body? The fact is that there are many members, but only one body.

Reflection

My wife and I did some decorating a while back. The room we were working on was gloomy, in need of a lift, so we decided to go for a creamy yellow. Decision made? Don't you believe it! The range of creamy yellows is unbelievable – 'Porcelain Bowl', 'Sunrise', 'Narcissus', 'Laughter', 'Buttermilk', 'Wicker', 'Ivory', 'Straw', to name but a few. These were all shades of yellow, yet they were all different, each with its own subtle nuance.

It doesn't take much to see where I'm going next, does it? Unity in diversity – what the Church is all about, or at least what it should be. We're all Christians – Anglican, Roman Catholic, Baptist, Methodist, Salvation Army, house church, and countless others – but we each have our own distinguishing characteristics. Within each denomination and individual fellowship, the same applies: an enormous variety of gifts, temperaments and experiences represented in every one of them. Is that a weakness? It can be, if we let it divide us, but it should be quite the opposite: a source of strength as we celebrate our unity in diversity. Imagine if there were just one shade of yellow – what an infinitely poorer place the world would be. So with the Church: we all profess Christ as Lord and all seek to follow him, but I doubt any two of us are the same. Thank God for that wonderful, astonishing and enriching diversity!

Prayer

Loving Father,
> teach me to celebrate the diversity of your Church
> and to rejoice in the variety you have given.

Help me to see differences not as a threat but as an opportunity,
> a chance to learn from others so that my faith may grow
> and deepen
> as I continue along my individual pathway of faith
> and on my pilgrimage together with others.

Amen.

77
Ephesians 2:19-21
United we stand

You, therefore, are no longer strangers and aliens, but fellow-citizens with the saints and members of God's family, established on foundations laid by the prophets and apostles with Jesus himself being the cornerstone. The whole edifice is held together by him, and it is he who helps us to become a temple, sacred and consecrated to God. Through him we are being joined together, God building a home for himself among us.

Reflection

Of what use is a single brick? Not very much. You could use it as a doorstop, perhaps, to displace water in your toilet cistern, or to stand a pot-plant on, but by and large a lone brick is of little value to anyone. A pile of bricks, however, is a different story. Then, if you've the inclination, your DIY skills can run riot. Why not build some steps, a wall, a barbecue? Even, if you've enough of them, a house! Well no, perhaps not, but you'll see what I mean. In my last garden I turned up so many isolated bricks while digging that I eventually had sufficient to let loose my creative juices and constructed a raised pond with an adjoining flowerbed which, as far as I know, is still standing today.

You'll no doubt have gathered where I'm heading with this, by now. It's not just bricks that belong together; people do too. We depend for our identity and happiness on the company of others. As John Donne so memorably put it, 'No man is an island'. For Christians that's especially true; Scripture repeatedly emphasises the importance of fellowship. 'Encourage one another', we're told; 'do not neglect to meet together'; 'bear one another's burdens'; and so we could continue. It's by no means impossible to be a Christian without going to church, but it's unquestionably harder attempting to go it alone. If we make time for others, for working and sharing together, listening and learning, our lives will be immeasurably enriched.

Prayer

When I'm tempted to go it alone, Lord,
   to neglect times of fellowship
   and follow you in isolation,
   remind me of my need for others.
Teach me that what's weak by itself
   is strong when brought together.
Amen.

SHROVE TUESDAY

Psalm 32:1-5

Something to celebrate?

Happy is the one whose wrongdoing is forgiven, whose faults are covered over. Happy are those to whom the Lord ascribes no guilt, and in whom there is no artifice. While I remained silent, my body grew weary with my constant groaning, for day and night your hand weighed heavily upon me; my strength dried up like sap in the heat of summer. Then I acknowledged my sin rather than attempting to conceal my guilt from you; I said, 'I will confess my disobedience to the Lord', and you absolved me from my guilt and wickedness.

Reflection

Mention Shrove Tuesday to my daughter and she immediately thinks of one thing: pancakes! They're one of her favourite meals, so this for her is a day to celebrate, to look forward to and to make the most of. When it was first instituted, centuries back, however, the mood it aimed to inculcate was rather different. It was designed as a solemn occasion, a time for sober reflection and earnest soul-searching; for recognising and confessing one's sins so that in the ensuing days of Lent one could strive to overcome them.

Which, then, is the right approach? Despite the Church's original intention, Shrove Tuesday swiftly became associated with fun and revelry, celebrated in some countries with carnivals, in others with parties and feasting, in others again with pancake races. Aware that Lent involves six weeks of self-denial, people were determined to indulge themselves before it started – to eat, drink and be merry. The rationale may be questionable, but they were right nonetheless to celebrate, for Lent, like every Christian season, should finally be about rejoicing. The clue as to why is in the word 'Shrove', from the Old English term 'shrive', meaning to hear confession and grant absolution. We acknowledge our sins in Lent not to brood upon them but to receive forgiveness. That's what God offers every one of us – pardon today, tomorrow and every day: something indeed truly worth celebrating!

Prayer

Loving God,
    help me to grasp more fully the breadth of your mercy
    and extent of your pardon,
        to understand that you do not seek to condemn or punish
        but delight rather to forgive,
        always being ready to wipe the slate clean
        and offer new beginnings.
Help me, then, to acknowledge my faults,
    not in despair over them
    but rejoicing at your grace,
    not dwelling on my weaknesses
    but exulting in the generosity of your love.
Amen.

LENT

TEMPTATION, SELF-EXAMINATION AND FORGIVENESS

79
Genesis 3:9-13
Original sin?

But the Lord God called out to the man, asking, 'Where are you?' The man replied, 'I heard you approaching in the garden, and because of my nakedness I was scared, so I concealed myself.' 'Who told you about being naked?' demanded God. 'Have you eaten fruit from the tree I told you to avoid?' The man answered, 'The woman whom you gave as a companion for me: she gave me some of its fruit, so I ate it.' Then the Lord God turned on the woman. 'What have you done?' he challenged her. The woman said, 'The serpent deceived me; that's why I ate.'

Reflection

The opening chapters of Genesis eloquently express God's pleasure and satisfaction in his creation, yet within just a few pages a very different picture emerges – a saga of human disobedience and rebellion in which the participants find themselves estranged both from God and from each other. In all this is a powerful portrayal of our human condition today: our potential for good compromised by our penchant for evil. So what went wrong? Where did God's plans come adrift, and why? How can we at one moment scale the heights and the very next plumb the depths? Part of the answer, at least, can be seen in Adam and Eve's attempts to justify their disobedience. 'It wasn't my fault,' they say. 'I was led astray.'

The tendency to blame others rather than ourselves is a universal human failing. Yet through downplaying our own culpability we make it easier to repeat our mistakes, wandering yet further astray from what God wants from us. It's easy to make excuses – we do it all the time to the point that we're often unaware of even doing so – but 99.9 per cent of the time they don't hold water. We are all accountable for our own actions; we can't dodge the issue. And should we try, we fail not only ourselves but God too, contributing a little more to despoiling his creation.

Prayer

Living God,
> there are times when my mistakes aren't entirely down to me –
> when I've been led astray by others or am a victim of circumstances –
> but usually my excuses are just an attempt to wriggle off the hook.

However much I wish it were otherwise, the fault lies with me,
> and so also does the responsibility.

Teach me that until I recognise my mistakes
> I cannot put them right
> or open my life to forgiveness.

Remind me that you are gracious,
> delighting to forgive and forget,
> and in that confidence may I approach you without dissemblance,
> truly sorry for all my sins.

Amen.

80
Psalm 19:12

Forgive our faults

Who among us can spot all our defects? Rid me of hidden faults.

Reflection

Look at the label on an electrical product or the like, and you'll usually find a reference to it having met strict quality control criteria and been passed fit for use. How it got through such purportedly stringent tests we sometimes wonder, for no sooner do we get the implement home and switch it on than the thing breaks! But, in theory at least, every such good we purchase should be in efficient working order, and any substandard item have been routinely discarded long before it reached the shelves.

What would happen, I wonder, if we were to be subjected to similar scrutiny, our lives measured against a checklist and consigned to the scrap heap if they failed to pass muster. In some ways, people experience just that, rejected on account of their gender, race, class or academic ability and condemned to the bottom of the pile. With God it's a different story. He does examine us, search our hearts and weigh our spirits, but though we repeatedly fall short, still he accepts us as we are, enough to die for us in Christ. He knows our faults but in his love he repeatedly mends our broken lives. For that astonishing truth, give thanks.

Prayer

Gracious God,
    though I fall short on innumerable counts,
    still you accept me as I am –
    enough to call me your child.
Thank you for that astonishing truth,
    and help me to serve you better,
    walking more faithfully the way of Christ.
Amen.

81
Psalm 26:2, 3
Examination time?

Examine me, O God, and search me; test my heart and mind. Test and confirm, O Lord, one way or the other who and what I am; search my heart and mind.

Reflection

Exams, they say, are getting easier. Is that true? Very possibly, but I'm glad nonetheless that for me the days of tests and such like are well and true over. Scribbling furiously for several hours in an examination hall, knowing that your whole future may depend on what you produce during that time, is a daunting prospect indeed – no less welcome than it's ever been. Some thrive under such conditions and are able to perform under pressure. A few have the happy knack of being able to cram in the required facts during an intensive spell of revision, even though they'll forget most of what they've learnt immediately after the exam. Others, however, despite having an excellent grasp of the subject in question, will go to pieces and end up failing miserably. The only advice we can give at such a time, and only fair expectation have of any examinee, is that they do their best.

Thankfully God doesn't ask us to sit exams, or demand that we meet a certain pass mark. He knows and understands our limitations and doesn't set impossible standards that we must somehow attain. The one thing he does ask, however, is that we're truly committed, serious about discipleship rather than simply playing at it. In that sense it's well worth asking God to examine us in order to help us understand where we're at: what progress we've made in faith; where our strengths and weaknesses lie; and what with his help we need to work at more carefully. He doesn't expect us to come out with flying colours, to be top of the class; he wants only to help us learn more of his ways, to know him better. If we give of our best in that, we can be sure God will make up what is lacking.

Prayer

Loving God,
    teach me that faith is not about passing a test
    but about completing the course,
    about what you have done
    rather than what I may do.
However often I fail you,
    remind me that your love continues
    and will never write me off.
Amen.

82
Psalm 38:18

I'm so sorry!

I confess my faults and am truly sorry for my mistakes.

Reflection

'Sorry for troubling you,' said the voice on the phone. 'Please give my apologies,' read the note to the meeting. 'I'm so sorry!' blurted out the pedestrian as he inadvertently bumped into a passer-by. We use the word 'sorry' in a host of ways without really meaning it. Truly saying sorry is altogether different. It involves swallowing our pride, overcoming hurt or anger and admitting we're wrong – and that is a much tougher proposition.

We do well to keep that in mind when it comes to acknowledging our faults before God. The gospel message of God's overflowing mercy can all too easily lead us to think 'It doesn't really matter what I do; God will forgive me.' But there's a flaw in such reasoning, for God's forgiveness depends on one thing: on us being *truly* sorry. It's not enough just to say the words, not sufficient merely to acknowledge our faults and confess our mistakes. We need to be genuinely remorseful and resolved to be different; in short, to say what we mean and mean what we say.

Prayer

Gracious God,
    I find it easy to say sorry to you,
        to acknowledge my weaknesses and confess my mistakes,
        but how much do my words really mean?
Help me fully to grasp that unless my apologies are real,
        backed up by genuine penitence and a true desire to change,
        they are little more than empty words.
Teach me not just to *say* sorry,
    but to mean it.
Amen.

83
Psalm 51:2, 7
Washed clean

Wash me carefully from my sins, and cleanse me from my faults. Sprinkle me with hyssop, and I will be clean; wash me, and I will become whiter than snow.

Reflection

What could be better sometimes than a refreshing hot shower? After a busy day, how good it feels to turn on the water and feel it taking away the grime, weariness and tensions of daily life. We emerge feeling clean, transformed and reinvigorated, almost as though we've washed inside as well as out.

With God it's not a question of 'almost'. When we open our lives to him and allow his love to wash over us, we are truly cleansed deep within; past mistakes are washed away as though they've never been. Not only this, but his grace is able to refresh us in body, mind and spirit; to renew faith, revitalise flagging commitment and restore strength and hope. Don't struggle wearily through life with the grime of past mistakes and failures sticking to you. Bathe in the grace of God revealed in Christ and step out each day, made new.

Prayer

Living God,
>full of grace and mercy,
>slow to punish and swift to pardon,
>thank you that I can put my faults and errors behind me;
>that you invite me to wash and be clean,
>to bathe in the immensity of your love and find forgiveness,
>a fresh start,
>day after day.

Open my life once more to your redeeming grace,
>and finish within me your new creation.

Amen.

84
Psalm 69:5

An unwitting mistake

You know my folly, O God; there can be no hiding my wrongs from you.

Reflection

'Robot Wars' pyjamas! – it was just what we were looking for, so we hung them on the pushchair and continued our look round the store. Some time later and several shops further on, we looked down in horror, for there were the pyjamas, still hanging where we'd put them earlier. Somehow, we'd paid for everything else but clean forgotten about these, walking away with them, security tag and all!

Luckily, I was able to rectify my mistake, hurrying back to the shop to settle up, but that experience brought home to me how easy it is inadvertently to make a mistake. A moment of carelessness, a word thoughtlessly spoken, or simply a case of sheer forgetfulness such as mine, and we can find we've done wrong though it was the last thing on our mind. Is it right to call such errors sin? Not in a pejorative, judgemental sense, no, yet unintended mistakes can be as destructive as any premeditated wrongdoing. They are also, by definition, the hardest mistakes to avoid, since we do not even know we are making them. Perversely, we can be harder on ourselves over our unintended blunders than God will ever be. Where he, as always, is ready to forgive, we chastise ourselves for not having seen the pitfalls. Such concern may be understandable and, if it helps avert repeating our errors, it has a place, but we will never eliminate every misjudgement from our lives. In this, as in everything, we depend on his grace – a grace that knows us and loves us as we are.

Prayer

Living God,
    forgive what I do
    and what I fail to do,
    what I am
    and what I fail to be.
For what I know to be wrong
    and for faults I haven't even begun to recognise,
    have mercy upon me.
Amen.

85
Psalm 103:8-12

Undeserved pardon

The Lord is merciful and gracious, abounding in steadfast love and not easily riled. He does not constantly accuse or forever nurse his anger, nor does he deal with us according to our sins or repay us for our mistakes. His unswerving love towards those that fear him is as great as the heavens are high above the earth; he banishes our faults from us as far as the east is from the west.

Reflection

Are sentences for serious crimes too lenient, and, if so, who's to blame? That question frequently rears its head in public debate and provokes heated response; politicians claim that judges are shirking their responsibilities, but the judiciary counter that its hands are tied. Probably the truth lies somewhere between the two positions, but what's undeniable is that judges, in the final analysis, have the responsibility of passing sentence within the guidelines set for them. They have to weigh up the evidence, together with any mitigating circumstances, and then pronounce accordingly, their remit being not to show mercy but to ensure, as far as possible, that justice is done.

How does that compare with God? On the one hand we believe him to be a God of justice, a God who one day will right wrongs and defeat evil. Yet, on the other, though he has more right than any to pronounce judgement, he delights to show mercy, this being the very essence of the gospel. None of us deserves his love or goodness; none has any right to a second chance, let alone countless others besides. We repeatedly go astray, flout his will and break his commandments, yet his nature is always to show pardon: to forgive and go on forgiving. There may be no justice in life, but thankfully there's no justice either, strictly understood, with God!

Prayer

Almighty God –
    all good, all true, all loving –
    your grace is too wonderful for me,
    your constant and undeserved pardon too awesome for words,
    but I thank and praise you for it,
    even as I struggle to take it in.
Teach me truly to understand the breadth of your mercy,
    and to live each day in the light of that knowledge,
    through Jesus Christ my Lord.
Amen.

86
Proverbs 28:13
A clean breast of it

No one who hides their mistakes will flourish, but whoever acknowledges and turns away from them will receive forgiveness.

Reflection

In the mid-1990s, an issue came to dominate British politics – the question of sleaze. Scarcely a week went by, it seemed, without some sordid scandal emerging about an MP or public figure; so much so that this matter in large part contributed to the humiliating defeat of the Conservative government in 1997. Countless prominent people had cause to wish they had come clean when they could, rather than have their guilty secrets splashed out later on the front pages of the tabloids. The reason they kept quiet, of course, was that they were afraid honesty might jeopardise their careers.

Fear can similarly come to rule *our* lives. The stakes involved may not be quite so high, but we hesitate to admit to past errors or present indiscretions for fear of losing face, endangering a relationship, or causing hurt to others and embarrassment to ourselves. At the time, sweeping a mistake under the carpet may seem an attractive option. It is only later that we learn how wrong we are, as guilt eats away at our conscience and the fear of being found out nags away at the back of our minds.

Saying sorry is never easy and can prove costly, but it is also the only way to resolution and reconciliation. Refusing to admit our mistakes may ultimately prove more costly still.

Prayer

Lord Jesus Christ,
    teach me to be honest with you,
    with myself
    and with others,
    and so may I know the peace of a clear conscience
    and a right relationship with all.
Amen.

87
Jeremiah 2:22
Made clean

Whatever soap you use, even if it were the most powerful imaginable, I would still be able to see the stain of your guilt showing through.

Reflection

One of my favourite parts of the country is Pembrokeshire. The coastline there is surely some of the best in all of Britain. Not only are there wonderful cliff walks and spectacular views; there are also some of the most perfect stretches of sand you could hope to find, a host of unspoilt bays and beaches. I say unspoilt, and it's true, but a relatively short time ago it was a different picture. The *Sea Empress* oil tanker was holed just outside Milford Haven on 15 February 1996, spilling its load along miles of coastline. Ecological damage was widespread but thankfully contained, due partly to the weather and partly to lessons that had been learnt during other such disasters.

There are times when our world seems hideously and hopelessly stained, not by an oil spill but by the unremitting torrent of human hatred, greed, pride, envy and downright folly. One problem ends, another begins; a wrong is righted only for another injustice to take its place. And so it continues; nothing, it seems, is able to eradicate our human weakness. That, though, is to reckon without God. He alone is able to cleanse from within, taking away what despoils our lives and bringing new beginnings. And through changing ordinary people like you and me, he can change others too. Open your heart, then, to his transforming touch, so that through you he may help to renew our world.

Prayer

Renew me, Lord –
  redeem and transform –
  for, like so many in this broken world,
  I am weak, faithless and foolish,
  repeatedly failing you.
Day by day, go on restoring and forgiving,
  so that, by your grace,
  I may become more fully the person you would have me be,
  and your kingdom may come closer on earth
  as it is in heaven.
Amen.

88
Micah 7:18, 19

The true picture

Who is like you, O God, ready to forgive sin? . . . Far from remaining angry for long, you take delight in showing mercy, forgiving iniquity and overlooking mistakes. Once more you will deal kindly with us; you will trample our mistakes underfoot and fling everything we've done wrong into the depths of the ocean.

Reflection

The *Mona Lisa* hit the news recently when it featured in the film *The Da Vinci Code*. Of course, one feature of the painting aroused controversy long before that: namely, the facial expression. Is it an enigmatic smile or a disapproving frown – what attitude did the artist intended to convey? Critics have debated the matter ad nauseam, yet they're no nearer reaching a consensus of opinion than they've ever been.

Equally, many people are uncertain what attitude to associate with God. Many see him as inherently judgemental, angered by our mistakes and disapproving of our weaknesses. Yet, to me, the Bible paints an overwhelmingly different picture, portraying God as patient and merciful, reluctant to punish and delighting to bless – a God who is full of compassion and swift to forgive. I may be wrong, of course, but the image of God that I get from Jesus in particular is not of a grim frown, nor in any way enigmatic, but quite simply one of a broad and welcoming smile, beaming out at us in love.

Prayer

Gracious God,
    help me to see you as you are
    rather than as I fear you to be;
    to grasp the wonder of your love and extent of your mercy.
Teach me that though *I* condemn, punish and despair of myself,
    you will never do the same;
    that the extent of my faults is matched by the breadth of
    your grace.
So them, this and every day,
    may I learn to celebrate your goodness that beams out upon me.
Amen.

89
Matthew 3:1, 2
Changing course

In those days John the Baptist appeared in the wilderness of Judea, proclaiming, 'Repent, for the kingdom of heaven has come near.' Then the people of Jerusalem and all Judea went out to him, and all the region along the Jordan, and they were baptised by him in the River Jordan, confessing their sins.

Reflection

Repent. It's not a word we use much nowadays, but there are few words that better express the message at the heart of the gospel. To become a Christian is not just about accepting a truth, confessing our faith in Christ. Nor is it simply an acknowledgement of wrongdoing and seeking of forgiveness. It is about a change of direction, a reorientation of life, pursuing a different course. That is the message at the heart of the gospel: that we need to turn from our old way to the way of Christ. For some that change, initially at least, may be more marked than others, their past lifestyle standing in stark contrast to their new-found faith, whereas those who have been brought up within the circle of the Church may find the outward change needed so negligible as to be almost imperceptible.

Repentance, though, is not a one-off thing – if only it were! We go on making mistakes every day of our life, inadvertently going astray with monotonous regularity. Before we know it, we are on the wrong road again; in all likelihood heading back the way we have come. Yet again, we find ourselves called to repent. The word may be archaic but the meaning is not. Whoever we are, whatever we have done, however many times we may have done so before, it is never too late to change course.

Prayer

Lord Jesus Christ,
    assure me that, however often I fail you,
    your patience is never exhausted,
    your love never withdrawn
    and your grace never denied.
Teach me that you long to forgive,
    waiting only for me to acknowledge my mistakes
    and come to you in true repentance.
Whenever, then, I lose my way,
    call me back
    and help me to walk with you once more in the way that leads
    to life.
Amen.

Matthew 4:1-4

A tempting prospect

After this the Spirit led Jesus into the desert so that the devil could tempt him. For forty days and nights he went without food, leaving him utterly famished. Then the tempter whispered in his ear, 'If you're God's Son, order these stones to become loaves of bread.' But Jesus replied, 'It is written, "We do not depend on bread alone for life, but on every word that proceeds from God's mouth."'

Reflection

For many, the season of Lent is synonymous with one thing: temptation. Specifically, it's associated with overcoming it: giving up some bad habit, perhaps; denying ourselves some luxury; or turning over a new leaf. The rationale for this is the time Jesus spent in the wilderness, during which he was tempted to turn stones into bread, to bow before Satan, and to test God by hurling himself off the highest pinnacle of the temple.

But what does all this actually mean for us today? Too often it's understood as a stick with which we should beat ourselves; an example of stern self-discipline that we must somehow follow, and God help us if we fail to do so. If Jesus could do it, the implication seems to be, then so also should we.

Yet is that really the point here? The temptation Jesus faced was to take the easy path rather than the hard, to fit in with the way of the world instead of walking the way of the cross. It's the fact that he refused to give in that gives us reason to hope and rejoice despite our faults. He took the road of costly self-sacrifice, the route that led to death, not because we deserve it but precisely because we don't, because he loves us as we are, warts and all. Lent speaks of the God who longs not to condemn but to forgive, not to punish but to bless.

Prayer

Lord Jesus Christ,
> forgive the ease with which I am led astray,
> the readiness with which I dilute my principles,
> the excuses with which I shut out your voice,
> preferring instead my own.

When I fall to temptation, help me to remember that *you* didn't,
> and to rejoice that your strength makes up for my weakness,
> your faithfulness for my many faults.

Amen.

91
2 Corinthians 13:5

Taking stock

Assess yourselves to check that you are living in the faith. Test yourselves to make sure. Do you not realise that Jesus Christ is in you? – assuming, of course, that your faith is not a sham.

Reflection

The very mention of the two words in our title today is enough to send a shiver down some people's spines. For them, stocktaking conjures up images of mad panic and frenetic activity; hours counting and recounting, scouring warehouses and checking manically through computer records, wondering just how so much has gone missing. For any business, though, taking stock is essential, not only in checking against theft and fraud but also in assessing how well and in what areas the firm is succeeding.

That is a principle we do well to apply to ourselves as Christians, as the words of Paul to the Corinthians powerfully remind us. 'Examine yourselves,' he says, 'and see whether you are living in the faith.' In other words, stop and take stock; make time for a long hard look at your life, some serious soul-searching. Don't just muddle through. Don't assume that everything is automatically ticking along as it should be. Don't imagine that once you've got the ball of Christian discipleship moving you can leave it to roll along smoothly by itself. Nothing could be further from the truth. It's all too easy to get lost along the way: to take a false step here, a wrong path there, until instead of making progress you're slipping backwards, unsure of where you're going and why. How far have you honoured the vows you once made? How far have you lived up to your commitment? How far have you achieved the things you once set out to achieve? In short, what have you made of your life? Stop and take stock. You may not like what you find, but at least you will know where you stand and, with God's help, have the chance to do something about it before it's too late to put matters right.

Prayer

Living God,
>   forgive me for being content to drift along in discipleship
>   with little sense of direction or purpose;
>   for assuming it is enough to get by,
>   and failing to ensure I do even that.

Teach me to take stock,
>   thoughtfully, honestly and prayerfully,
>   and to see myself as I really am
>   rather than as I imagine myself to be.

Amen.

92

James 3:2a

A second chance

We all make many mistakes.

Reflection

I was playing a game of chess and saw what looked to be a winning move, so I reached out and played it instinctively without stopping to think it through. Almost immediately I realised I'd blundered – but would my opponent spot it? Unfortunately the answer was yes, and suddenly I found myself in deep trouble, struggling to stay in the game. Had it been a friendly I could possibly have taken my move back, but this was a competition with no such luxury allowed. I'd made my mistake and had to live with it.

So often in life there's no going back. We make a blunder and people pounce upon it, or an error of judgement that has repercussions greater than anything we ever imagined. Try as we might, we can't undo the damage and have another stab at things. But with God it's different. No matter how often we go wrong he's ready to give us a second chance. Whatever mistakes we've made, we can put them behind us and start afresh through his grace, so long as we truly acknowledge our fault and yearn to move on. Don't suffocate under a weight of remorse. Receive the forgiveness God delights to offer and begin again.

Prayer

Gracious God,
    teach me that though I cannot put the clock back and undo what's been done,
    I can nonetheless put the past behind me and move on;
    that you are always ready to give me a second chance,
    wiping out my mistakes as though they have never been.
Whatever my blunders, then,
    whatever my faults,
    give me faith in your transforming power
    and the future you hold in store.
Amen.

SACRIFICE AND SELF-DENIAL

93

Proverbs 14:21, 31

Sharing our plenty

Those who spurn their neighbours sin against God, whereas those who show kindness to the poor will themselves find true happiness. Those who exploit the poor insult their maker, but those who respond to the needy do him honour.

Reflection

It was a busy day, with no time to prepare a proper meal, so we decided to make do with a bowl of soup. Not much, we thought, but it would get us by, and we could always make up for it with a snack later. But, that night, a news item concerning soup kitchens set up for Christmas caught our eye, bringing home the stark fact that, for many, a bowl of soup is not a makeshift stand-in but a luxury, a rare hot meal to be savoured. It's the same for countless others across the world, millions not having the first idea where their next meal is coming from. For them, 'getting by' would do very nicely.

Interestingly, soup features in a small but simple symbolic response to the scandal of world poverty and injustice: the so-called 'hunger lunch'. You'll no doubt have encountered the idea and probably have participated in such a lunch yourself. Instead of having your usual midday or evening meal, you have bread and soup (or perhaps cheese), and you give what you would otherwise have spent to a charity like Oxfam or Christian Aid. Such lunches are not, of course, going to change the world by themselves, but they're a start, and if we were all to get into the habit of denying ourselves more regularly and donating the money saved to a good cause, we would certainly make an impact, perhaps even a significant difference. Have we the commitment, love and compassion to occasionally go without so that others needn't go hungry?

Prayer

God of all,
> though I briefly respond to the plight of the poor,
> too often I forget that their need continues;
> that poverty and hunger are endemic to our world,
> part of an order that I'm complicit in maintaining.

Give me genuine compassion,
> a real desire to make a difference,
> and help me –
> as part of my response –
> to be willing to have a little less
> so that others may have at least a little.

Amen.

94
Matthew 5:40-42
That little bit extra

'If anyone decides to sue you and take your coat, let them have your cloak as well, and whoever forces you to go one mile, go with them a second also. Give to whoever begs, and do not turn away anyone wishing to borrow from you.'

Reflection
If you've ever tried reading something in Hebrew you'll know that, initially, it's a strange experience. Why? Because the language is very different from our own; the words start on the right-hand side of the page and are read right to left – in other words, from a Western perspective, backwards. A book, similarly, starts on what we would consider the last page and ends on the 'first'. All very confusing, though to a Jewish reader, of course, it's us, rather than them, who have got things muddled.

At Lent, likewise, there's a danger of approaching things the wrong way round, seeing it exclusively as a time of self-denial. That's certainly a part of it, epitomised by the time Jesus spent in the wilderness, but he renounced the world there in order to commit himself to it, accepted a challenge as much as resisted temptation. That's what he asks of us, too. The emphasis in discipleship is on going the extra mile, doing not just what's asked or expected but more besides. In other words, it's more about what we *can* do than what we *can't*. So what does that mean in practice? The possibilities are endless. It may be, this Lent, that God wants us simply to commit ourselves more firmly to Christ. Or perhaps he's asking us to take on some extra responsibility, to respond to a sense of calling, to get more involved in our local community, to help a neighbour, to support some cause, to show concern for a friend, to give more generously. Whatever it is, Lent means more than merely giving something up. Above all, it's about taking something on.

Prayer

Living God,
>   save me from turning this season into a negative one,
>   concerned simply with sacrifice and self-denial.

Help me to make it positive as well:
>   an opportunity to put faith into practice,
>   to offer you something extra as an expression of my love and loyalty.

Teach me to think about not just what I shouldn't do
>   but what I *should*;
>   not just what I can't do
>   but what I *can*;
>   and help me to grasp the opportunity to serve,
>   this and every day.

Amen.

Matthew 6:16-18

Parading our virtue

'Whenever you fast, don't emulate hypocrites by putting on a long face and sanctimonious expression to ensure that everyone knows all about your piety. Note this, the only reward those acting in such a way can look forward to is the self-righteous satisfaction they've already enjoyed. In stark contrast, when you fast, spruce yourself up as you would for a feast, anoint your head with oil and wash your face, so that the only one who knows you're fasting is your Father, who knows your innermost thoughts and will reward you accordingly.'

Reflection

Somewhere near my home lives a budding trumpeter. I'm not sure where exactly – it may be in any one of a number of streets – but they're definitely somewhere fairly close by. How do I know this? Because if the weather is warm, I hear the sound of their playing drifting across on the breeze, and very pleasant it is too. As to whether this budding Louis Armstrong is aware of how far the sound of their instrument carries, who can say – my guess is they'd be mortified had they any idea – but the near neighbourhood is regularly given the opportunity to monitor their progress. Perhaps, in time, we'll be holding up placards giving marks out of ten, *Strictly Come Dancing* style!

We may not all be musicians, but most of us are naturals when it comes to blowing our own trumpets. Given the chance to broadcast some success, we just can't help ourselves. There's nothing wrong, of course, with a healthy pride in our achievements; what Jesus censured in his words above is something rather different: parading our virtue in public. None of us have any justification for that, for our lives repeatedly fall short of what they ought to be. Even if it were otherwise, there would still be no place for showy discipleship. Faith must show itself in action, certainly, but it must do so without seeking attention, without fuss, without any other aim than to respond simply and sincerely to him.

Prayer

Loving God,
    save me from outward piety,
    from any suggestion of smugness, bigotry or hypocrisy.
Instead of parading my virtue,
    may I learn the secret of unassuming discipleship,
    so that I may serve you with no hidden agenda,
    my only desire being to love and honour you.
Amen.

96
Matthew 6:19-21

Lasting treasure

'Do not amass earthly treasures for yourselves, which are vulnerable to attack by moths or rust, or to thieves breaking in and making off with them. Instead, accrue treasures in heaven, which are vulnerable neither to moth, rust nor burglary. For you can be sure of this; wherever your treasure is to be found, your heart will be found too.'

Reflection

My brother had been waiting for the interview for weeks – an important one that, if successful, would lead to an exciting new job – but when he came the evening before to try on his best suit it was to discover, to his horror, that it had been attacked by moths and was full of gaping holes. There was nothing for it other than for him to rush out the next morning and buy a new suit. Happily, despite the rush involved, the interview proved successful.

It's not just clothes that can suffer from the passage of time. Food quickly grows stale, medicines have their shelf lives, books start to yellow, metal turns rusty, gadgets wear out, and so forth. What seems new and bright today swiftly becomes old and faded, frequently far too rapidly for comfort. That's not to say we shouldn't enjoy such things while we can, but Jesus reminds us that we shouldn't pin all our happiness upon anything in this world, no matter how special it may be, for, in this life, all good things come to an end. We can't seal happiness in a box and store it away. Rather, we must celebrate while we have it. Most of all, though, we must recognise that lasting fulfilment and unfading joy lie beyond this world entirely – in the things of God that will neither fade nor perish.

Prayer

Gracious God,
> thank you that though all else fades away, your love continues –
> unchanging,
> unshakable,
> unending.

Give me wisdom, then, truly to celebrate your gifts
> but never to pin my entire well-being upon them;
> to seek treasure in heaven
> as well as pleasure on earth.

Amen.

97
Luke 9:23, 24

The cost of discipleship

He said to all, 'If any want to come after me, let them deny themselves and take up their cross daily, and then follow me. For those wishing to save their life will lose it, but those who lose their life for my sake will save it.'

Reflection

'I'm delighted to tell you that you've won a free holiday in our prize draw competition.' Have you had a phone call like that recently? It's sales talk, of course; just one of the many marketing ploys used to convince us that we're getting something for nothing, whereas, in fact, the opposite is more likely true. Another tack is the one sometimes employed by book and music clubs: 'Buy any four for 99 pence each', only we then have to buy another four at full price during the next year.

It's easy to be swept along by wonderful-sounding promises, without stopping to consider the commitment entailed. In terms of the Christian faith, though, there should be no such danger, for Jesus never attempted to conceal the real cost of discipleship. If you want the reward, he tells us, there's a price to pay. To get something out of faith we must also put something in. There is no sales hype, no dressing things up with fantastic offers, yet the irony is that in this case the price is more than worth paying!

Prayer

Lord Jesus Christ,
    I find it hard to deny myself even a little,
    let alone to give my all.
There is so much I want to enjoy,
    so much I want to achieve,
    and the thought of sacrificing any of that is one I would rather push aside.
Yet you have taught that it is in losing life that we truly find it,
    and that lasting treasures are found not on earth but in heaven.
Help me, then, instead of clinging slavishly to self-interest,
    to give of myself freely,
    just as you gave yourself for me.
Amen.

98
Colossians 2:20—3:2
A positive response

If you died with Christ to the spirits underlying the universe, how is it that you behave as though you still belong to the world? Why do you give in to regulations such as, 'Hands off! Don't taste! Not to be touched'? Regulations like these are concerned with perishable goods and are simply conventions rooted in human instructions and institutions. They may look astute in terms of advancing self-imposed godliness, modesty and mortification of the flesh, but they are useless in preventing decadence. If, then, you have been raised to new life with Christ, pursue the things of heaven, where Christ is ensconced at the right hand of God. Focus on what is above, not on the things of this world.

Reflection

What does the season of Lent mean to you? What sort of ideas does it conjure up in your mind? For many, it is associated with giving something up: an opportunity, perhaps, to kick that unwanted habit, go at last on that long-intended diet, or deny oneself those unnecessary extra luxuries. All such acts of discipline have their place, as the teaching of Jesus concerning taking up our cross makes clear, but they give a very one-sided view of Lent, for, if anything, it should be about taking something on; committing yourself, in the words of Jesus, to going the extra mile.

That doesn't mean taking work on for work's sake, or looking for extra duties, demands and responsibilities. Rather, it is about resolving to follow Christ more faithfully, determined to give him our whole-hearted discipleship. It might mean more disciplined devotion, perhaps more practical service, maybe more effective witness or possibly the offering of previously unused gifts.

Whatever it is, it is more than giving something up; it is primarily giving something back to the one who gave us his all. Consider today what Christ has done for you; then ask what you can do for him, and use Lent as an opportunity to respond.

Prayer

Living God,
> save me from slipping into a faith of negatives;
> from imagining you are more concerned with what I shouldn't do
> than with what I should.

Teach me that although there is a vital place in discipleship for self-denial
> there is also a place for affirming and celebrating life in all its fullness.

Help me, then, to use this season of Lent as a time to grow and learn,
> to deepen my faith and strengthen my commitment;
> above all, to make more room for you.

Amen.

STILLNESS AND QUIETNESS

99
Genesis 2:2
Take a break

On the seventh day God completed the work he'd been busy with; on that day he rested from all his exertions.

Reflection

The film was about to begin, but first the usual message came over the Tannoy, asking the audience to switch off their mobile phones: a simple act of courtesy to ensure that everyone could enjoy their evening. Sadly, not everybody could bring themselves to oblige; several people continued to text throughout the film and one even took a call. Inconsiderate though that may be, it probably won't surprise you. Try chatting to almost any young person today, and the chances are that their phone will be beeping in the background indicating a text, Facebook or Twitter message coming through. While one eye may be on you, the other will be constantly straying back to their screen.

It's not just phones that need switching off; it's us too sometimes, both for our benefit and for that of others. We may think we can keep on going for ever – that our staying power is limitless and our energy unlike that of anyone else – but of course we can't; we all finally need a break for the sake of our health and sanity. Fail to switch off and the consequences can be more serious than we realise; even, perhaps, mental or physical breakdown as our bodies finally force us to rest. And it's not just us who suffer but our nearest and dearest as well; they, all too often, have to bear the brunt of our preoccupation and fatigue. Surely one of the points of the creation story where it speaks of God resting is that if work is sacred, so too is leisure, both being integral to fullness of life. So then, whatever it is you're switched on to, and however important or worthwhile it may seem, remember sometimes to switch off, before damage is done.

Prayer

Almighty God,
>   teach me to appreciate the importance of being still,
>   of taking a breather from the demands of life,
>   however pressing they may be.

Save me from having no time to pause and ponder,
>   from allowing the affairs of daily life so to dominate
>   that I lose sight of what really counts.

Show me the difference between doing enough and doing too much,
>   and help me to get the balance right.

Amen.

100

Psalm 39:5

What's the hurry?

You have made the days of my life like a few hand spans, the time allotted to me being barely anything in your perspective.

Reflection

It was the Horse of the Year Show again, and the riders were racing against the clock, striving to save the few seconds that would mean the difference between success and failure. The faster they tried to go, the more mistakes they made, fence poles clattering to the ground as their mounts got caught mid-stride. It was a classic example of the old saying 'More haste, less speed'.

In life we can be equally conscious of the clock ticking by, increasingly coming to see time as an enemy. The temptation, as a result, is to try to fill each moment with frantic activity. To do that, though, risks turning our time on earth into a mad race rather than a joyful celebration. God calls us to view life from a different perspective: that of eternity rather than of our brief mortal span. Whatever joys you have now they are as nothing compared to those yet to come. So then, next time you catch yourself rushing about like a headless chicken, pause and learn to do things in God's time rather than your own, remembering that, through his grace, you have all the time in the world . . . and beyond!

Prayer

Eternal God,
 teach me that though this life will one day finish,
 life with you will continue,
 and the joys you hold in store will never come to an end.
Help me, then, in that assurance,
 to put aside my running against the clock
 and to rejoice in the here and now,
 having time for me,
 for you
 and for others.
Amen.

Ecclesiastes 3:1-8

A time and a place

There is a season for everything, and a time for every activity under heaven: a time to be born and a time to die; a time to plant and a time to uproot; a time to kill and a time to heal; a time to pull down and a time to build up; a time to cry and a time to laugh; a time to grieve and a time to dance; a time to scatter stones and a time to gather them; a time to embrace and a time not to embrace; a time to seek and a time to lose; a time to keep and a time to throw away; a time to tear and a time to mend; a time for silence and a time for speech; a time to love and a time to hate; a time for war and a time for peace.

Reflection

One of the ways I've found time to write as much as I have done has been by carrying a Dictaphone with me on my lunchtime walks so that I can record ideas as I go along. The other day, however, the batteries ran out almost as soon as I set off, so I strolled for a change with my thoughts focused on the things around me: the sound of birds in the trees and sheep in the field, the feel of the sun and the breeze, the sight of flowers growing by the roadside, hedgerows bursting into leaf and clouds drifting overhead, the smell of the grass and spring blossom. I realised suddenly how often I pass such things by without taking them in, my mind so preoccupied with other matters that I overlook the countless blessings that daily surround me.

We can all make that mistake. Perhaps we're too busy rushing from one thing to the next, perhaps we're fretting over a problem, perhaps familiarity has inured us to the wonders that surround us, or perhaps simply our minds are elsewhere. Whatever the reason, we can fail to celebrate the present moment. For our physical, emotional and spiritual well-being we all need occasionally simply to pause and ponder, to stop for a moment and reflect on the many reasons we have to be thankful. We can't do that all the time, of course, because life inevitably puts demands on our time and attention, but we fail to do it at all at our peril. As the book of Ecclesiastes reminds us, there's a time and a place for everything.

Prayer

Living God,
>too often I stumble through life with my eyes closed
>and fail to take in the beauty and wonder of this world you have given.

Distracted by daily responsibilities,
>I forget to rejoice in the here and now,
>to count my blessings and celebrate the given moment.

Teach me that there is a time and a place for everything,
>including quiet reflection –
>time to still my soul and take stock;
>to let go of the concerns that press upon me and simply to be.

Save me from being so preoccupied with the business of living
>that I have no time truly to live.

Amen.

102
Ecclesiastes 4:6
Quiet contentment

A quiet and contented handful is preferable to two handfuls won through constant toil and striving vainly after wind.

Reflection

The chances are that you'll be taking a holiday around this time of year, particularly if you're a parent with children at school and thus constrained in the dates you can choose. Whether it's a few days' break or rather longer, time away does us good, providing us with the opportunity for much-needed refreshment; a chance to forget work, the household chores and the daily routine for a while and to recharge our batteries. Without such opportunities to relax and unwind, our health would eventually suffer, physically as well as mentally. We all need time to pause and ponder – to appreciate such simple pleasures as flowers in bloom and birds in song, the scent of the sea and caress of the breeze.

I could move on from this to talk of the need for prayer and reflection, for quiet time set apart for God, and it would be a valid point, for we can all too easily forget the importance of such times. But the writer of Ecclesiastes, in the verses above, is talking simply of the need we all share for respite from the demands of each day; the importance of pausing occasionally and taking stock; the value of simply stopping, if only briefly, to drink in the world around us. Rush around from this to that and, in the long run, we'll pay the price in terms of peace of mind and inner well-being. Whatever we seem to get from it, more will be lost. Make time for God, definitely, but make time also for yourself, and give yourself, when necessary, the break you need.

Prayer

Loving God,
    too often I fret about what must be done,
    worry over this or that,
    turn over problems in my mind, and so forth.
Give me the patience, discipline and discernment I need to switch
    off sometimes;
    to let go,
    empty my thoughts
    and be still,
    so that I may find inner refreshment
    and real peace.
Amen.

103

Isaiah 30:15

Slow down

This is what the living God, the Holy One of Israel says: 'Return to me and find your salvation in being still, for in rest and quietness lies true strength', but you just weren't interested in listening.

Reflection

One of the bugbears for motorists today is the ever-increasing number of speed bumps in our towns and cities. I speak from personal experience; just about every route to the town centre from my home seems to have been designed to shake loose as many nuts and bolts as possible. As the car suspension takes yet another pounding, it's hard sometimes not to question the wisdom of the powers that be, but, of course, however unwelcome traffic-calming devices may seem, they are installed for a purpose: to slow drivers down so as to make residential areas that little bit safer for pedestrians. Let's face it, we can all on occasions be tempted to drive faster than we ought to, and if speed bumps help to save even one life or prevent an ugly accident they've more than served their purpose.

In life, as much as on the road, we can be in too much of a hurry sometimes. For all our labour-saving devices, we live today at a more hectic pace than ever before, always feeling under pressure and striving to cram that little bit extra into the unforgiving minute. But are we happier for it? Probably the opposite is true; many today feel stressed and overloaded, and crave some respite in which to pause and get their bearings. We all need time to unwind, to reflect on what we're doing and why – above all, time for God. That's why God's advice in the verse above is so important, for unless we learn to be still in his presence we will lose sight of what really matters, and all our hustle and bustle will count finally for nothing.

Prayer

Lord Jesus Christ,
    whenever I forget you,
    believing I have more important things to do,
    more pressing concerns to see to,
    remind me that you hold the words of eternal life,
    the answer to my inner hunger and deepest needs.
In my list of daily priorities,
    help me to set time aside for you *first*,
    not *last*.
Amen.

104
Matthew 14:22, 23

A time to be still

He persuaded his disciples to board the boat and cross to the other side ahead of him, while he dismissed the crowds, and having done that, he went up the mountain by himself to pray. As evening fell, he was there alone.

Reflection

We watched spellbound as it appeared out of the undergrowth, making its way cautiously up the lawn to the supply of food left out for it in anticipation. It was our first, and so far only, sighting of a badger in the wild, and the few minutes we spent watching it feed made it a holiday to remember. I could have watched for longer, but as I shifted position to get a better view, it caught sight of my movement and, in a trice, it was gone. Watching wildlife requires stillness and patience, the ability to stay quiet for some length of time. Fail to do that, and the object of our search remains hidden, tantalisingly out of sight.

There are parallels here with glimpsing God, although we should not push the analogy too far. He is with us all the time, everywhere at every moment, yet most of the time we are unaware of it, too caught up in the hustle and bustle of life. It is often only when we pause for a few moments, making time to be still and reflect, that the full wonder of his presence dawns on us. Even Jesus, who seems to have been in tune with God throughout his life, recognised the need to draw aside from the crowds and spend a quiet time in prayer. If Jesus needed such times to focus his thoughts on God, how much more do we need them in turn!

Prayer

Living God,
 teach me to create space in my life for you,
  to make a few moments every day in which I can be quiet and still.
And teach me to do that not as an afterthought
 but as a prerequisite,
  recognising that when I give you your proper place,
  everything else will fit into place as well.
Amen.

105
Mark 6:31

A quiet place

'Come somewhere quiet', he told them, 'and spend time with me by yourselves, finding rest.'

Reflection

One of the things I like about London is its many parks. I don't just mean the large and famous ones, but also the innumerable small and leafy squares that dot the capital, each providing an oasis of tranquillity amid the stresses and strains of city life. One moment you can be walking past skyscrapers, offices, main roads and teeming crowds, and the next you're sitting quietly listening to the song of a blackbird, watching squirrels scurry from tree to tree or admiring the well-stocked flowerbeds, rich in scent and colour. Such places provide a welcome lunchtime retreat for thousands of workers, an opportunity to pause and recharge their batteries or simply to get things in perspective.

Whoever we are, we all need times like those – moments simply to be quiet and reflect. They afford an opportunity for God to speak to us and to offer his help, guidance, correction or challenge. Not, of course, that he can't speak elsewhere – quite the contrary – but often it's only when we take a breather from the humdrum business of daily life that we realise how he's been present and what he's been saying all along. Take time to get away from it all, if only briefly, and you will find yourself reinvigorated – ready to return to the world and serve God there once more.

Prayer

Gracious God,
> however rushed I may be,
> however many the demands put upon me,
> help me always to remember that you are God,
> the one who alone gives true meaning to all I do,
> to life itself.

In drawing aside from the world may I glimpse you more fully within it,
> and may time spent with you transform my approach to time itself.

Amen.

106

Mark 6:45, 46

Stepping back, stepping forward

He told his disciples to get into the boat and go on ahead of him to Bethsaida, on the other side, while he dismissed the crowd. After taking leave of them, he went up on the mountain to pray.

Reflection

Have you ever heard of Henry the Hermit or St Cuthbert? Both are associated with the magical coast of Northumberland. St Cuthbert made his home on Lindisfarne, otherwise known as Holy Island – a small rocky outcrop connected to the mainland by a narrow causeway that for most of the day is submerged by the sea. Henry was even more of a recluse, spending his days in prayer and meditation on an island some distance offshore.

Few of us will feel called to quite such an austere way of life, but we can learn something from their example, for there are times when we too need to get away from it all, if only for a few moments, in order to hear God's voice. It's not that he's removed from the daily round of life – far from it – but sometimes pressures can build up in such a way that they obscure his presence. When writing my books, for example, there have been many times when I struggled for inspiration, becoming increasingly agitated when none was forthcoming. At one time, I would have soldiered on regardless, spending hours and even a whole day on one paragraph, yet getting nowhere. Experience, though, has taught me to get up and walk away; to take a stroll in the garden, or to reflect on a different passage, or simply to spend a few moments doing nothing. Through stepping back, I am able to step forward.

It is noticeable that Jesus himself, at key moments in his life, made time for quietness, drawing away from the crowds, spending time alone high in the hills so that he could focus on the presence of God, away from the innumerable pressures and demands put upon him. It is not always easy to do that, I know. When the children are screaming and there's a pile of washing-up to see to, when there's another meeting to attend and another deadline to meet, stepping back can seem a luxury we can ill afford. Yet, the fact is, it is a necessity; a step we sometimes need to make if we are to have any hope of progressing further.

Prayer

Living God,
> teach me to find time for you each day,
> if only for a few moments,
> so that I may hear your voice and discern your will.

Teach me to step back and take stock,
> so that I may then step forward,
> renewed in faith,
> strengthened in spirit,
> and equipped for whatever you may ask,
> in Jesus' name.

Amen.

107
Luke 10:40-42

A pause for thought

Martha was preoccupied with her many tasks; so she came to him and asked, 'Lord, doesn't it matter to you that my sister has left me to do all the work by myself? Tell her to lend a hand.' But the Lord answered her, 'Martha, Martha, you are fretting and distracted by many things; only one thing is really important. Mary has chosen that more important thing, and it will not be taken away from her.'

Reflection

We live today at breakneck speed, rushing here, there and everywhere, yet forever chasing our tails. Despite having labour-saving gadgets such as our grandparents could only have dreamed of, we are part of a society ravaged by exhaustion and burn-out as we attempt to cram yet more activity into our already overcrowded lives. The material rewards are many, yet spiritually most of us are hopelessly impoverished.

We need sometimes to pause and ask ourselves where we are going and why. We need to consider the deeper things of life and to reflect on what actually matters most. Unless we pause to think now, we may reach the end of our days only to discover that we have frittered our lives away on much that is ultimately empty and meaningless trivia.

Prayer

Lord of all,
    I have made time and space for quietness to hear your voice.
Go with me now into the turmoil of life,
    with all its noise and confusion,
    all its demands and responsibilities,
    and may your peace rest with me there,
    this day and for evermore.
Amen.

SPIRITUAL GROWTH

108

Psalm 92:12-14

Freshening up

Those who honour God will thrive and flourish – like a palm tree or cedar of Lebanon. Because they are planted in the Lord's house they will bloom in his courts, continuing to bear fruit into old age and remaining fresh and green.

Reflection

During my years spent in pastoral visiting I was frequently offered some kind of refreshment. Sometimes that was hugely welcome, but not always, for frequently the cake or biscuits offered were so stale as to be inedible. They looked all right, but the first mouthful swiftly proved otherwise, to the point that I became a dab hand at surreptitiously concealing various foodstuffs in my pockets and discreetly disposing of them on my way home afterwards. A mouldering layer of crumbs about my person seemed to be one of the occupational hazards of ministry!

We can't keep *anything* fresh indefinitely, and that includes our faith; like so much else in life, it runs the danger of growing stale with the passage of time. But just as we can use a fridge, freezer or biscuit tin to preserve the life of food, so we can take steps in terms of our commitment. We can start by reading the Bible regularly, not just passages we're familiar with but those we've passed by, for each is able to open up new horizons. We can spend more time in prayer, not simply following the same old format but exploring the rich heritage of past and present, allowing the language and ideas of others to breathe new life into a familiar practice. We can share with other Christians and on occasions visit churches of different traditions, as these too are able to offer a fresh perspective on truths we've come to know so well. Above all, of course, we can simply make quality time for God in which to consider again what he means for us today. Fail to do that, and though our faith may still look the part to others, we may well find it's gone horribly stale just when its freshness is most needed.

Prayer

Living God,
    my faith is not what it could or should be.
Instead of renewing it each day,
    I allow it grow stale,
    no longer fit for purpose.
Instead of refreshing it through time spent with you and putting
    it into practice,
    I put it to one side,
    often forgetting it altogether, so that it moulders slowly away.
Forgive me, and revitalise my commitment.
Breathe new life into my spirit and fresh enthusiasm into my heart,
    so that love for you may be born anew in me each day.
Come now and restore what is lacking,
    through Jesus Christ my Lord.
Amen.

109
Proverbs 1:5-7
Words of wisdom

Let those who are wise hear more and increase in learning; let those with insight acquire skill in understanding proverbs and sayings, the teachings of the wise and their conundrums. Fearing God is where knowledge begins; the foolish loathe wisdom and instruction.

Reflection

If I were to ask you to list ten proverbs, which, I wonder, would you come up with? 'Too many cooks spoil the broth', perhaps? 'Many hands make light work'? 'A rolling stone gathers no moss'? 'A bird in the hand is worth two in a bush'? 'A stitch in time saves nine'? All of us, I suspect, will have our personal favourites, a host of proverbs having been handed down across the centuries, many of them known to us since childhood, and each encapsulating important truths about life. A proverb is able, in a few words and with the minimum of fuss, not only to set us thinking about deep truths but also to provide profound answers.

Little wonder, then, that proverbs have proven so popular. And they've done so not just in popular tradition but also in Scripture, above all in the books of Proverbs and Ecclesiastes. Those are two of the most unusual books of the Bible but few are able to speak more directly about daily life. Put together, we're told, by King Solomon, famed of course for his wisdom, they include words of advice concerning just about anything and everything: money, marriage, work, leisure, honesty, corruption, greed, generosity, words, deeds, and much, much more. Together they offer a hard-headed realism coupled with firm faith and, most importantly, a conviction that the two belong inseparably together. Why not build them into your daily devotions, perhaps reading just one verse a day and pondering quietly on its message and how it applies to you today? Solomon understood the wisdom of seeking insight and understanding? What about you?

Prayer

Almighty God,
>   not only do you tell me in Scripture to seek wisdom,
>   but you provide there tools to help me do it,
>   words offering food for thought and guidance for daily life.

Teach me to make time both to read and to reflect on what
>   these say,
>   genuinely seeking enlightenment as to the path I should take
>   and the decisions I should make.

Help me to understand how little I know
>   and how much I still have to learn,
>   and give me patience, humility and diligence to study
>   your word
>   so that I might live life wisely
>   and truly walk the way of Christ.

Amen.

110
Isaiah 55:1, 2

Food for our souls

Pay attention, everyone who is thirsty, come and find water; and you that have no food, come, buy and eat! Come, buy wine and milk, not for money but beyond price. Why spend your money on that which is not bread, and why offer your labour for that which cannot satisfy? Listen carefully to what I say, and you will eat what is good, delighting yourselves in the richest of food.

Reflection

One of the hardest aspects of parenting must surely be getting one's children to eat. Offer them a bar of chocolate or a bag of sweets and there's no problem, but give them a healthy balanced meal and they will sit there picking at it for all the world as though you're trying to poison them! Sometimes we just don't know what's good for us, whether we're children or otherwise.

When it comes to nourishing our souls, we all tend to be addicted to junk food rather than that which can truly satisfy. We cram so much into our lives in an effort to find fulfilment, yet still cannot fill the aching void deep inside. It's nothing new: countless generations have done the same since time immemorial. As the prophet Isaiah knew all too well, we are hopelessly addicted to instant satisfaction; to that which instinctively appeals to our senses yet cannot begin to meet our innermost needs. We need to make time for God, space for prayer and reflection, and room in our lives for spiritual sustenance. Fail to do that and, though our stomachs may be full to overflowing, our emaciated souls will slowly starve within us.

Prayer

Living God,
>   you tell me that those who hunger and thirst after
>   righteousness shall be filled.

Teach me the secret of such hunger.

Teach me to empty myself so that I may be filled by you;
>   to desire your kingdom,
>   seek your will
>   and study your word,
>   earnestly,
>   eagerly,
>   expectantly.

Nourish me through your word,
>   nurture me through your grace,
>   feed me through your Spirit
>   and fill me with your love.

Amen.

111
Hosea 6:3
Keep moving

Let us know the Lord; let us press on so that we might know him.

Reflection

When I was a boy I remember being fascinated by the travelators that led to many of the deep tube lines on the London Underground. These were no everyday escalators, the sort you might find in a department store or shopping mall. No, they were altogether different: long, flat moving walkways that seemed to go on for ever, transporting a bustling throng effortlessly to and from the station platforms. Some people strolled purposefully along these contraptions, intent on beating the queue, but most seemed happy simply to stand still and be carried along.

In Christian discipleship, sometimes, we can act as though we have access to some kind of spiritual travelator. No effort is required on our part, we seem to think, to help us progress in our journey of faith. We can simply leave it to God to take us where we need to go. So long as we've stepped on to the walkway, so to speak, the rest is down to him. The reality, of course, is that we couldn't be more wrong. Yes, we depend ultimately on his grace. Yes, we need him to help us change. But that doesn't mean we can stand idly by. As Hosea reminds us, we need to press on, doing our bit if we would truly know God and serve him better. That means working at our faith and seeking each day to walk more fully in it. It means doing whatever we can to deepen our relationship with God and help it to grow. He's there to help us along the way, but if we expect him to carry us entirely we're in for a disappointment, and will end up getting nowhere.

Prayer

Living God,
    too often I'm casual in commitment,
    lackadaisical,
    apathetic,
    only occasionally working at my relationship with you
    and most of the time barely giving it a second thought.
Teach me to yearn to know you better
    and to step out in faith,
    pressing on to make such knowledge mine.
Amen.

Mark 8:29-33

An evolving faith

He said to them, 'What about you – who do you say that I am?' Peter answered, 'You are the Christ.' Then he warned them to tell no one about him. And he began to teach them that it was necessary for the Son of Man to suffer many things, to be rejected by the chief priests, the elders and the scribes, to be killed and on the third day to rise again. He made no secret of it. Then Peter, taking him aside, began to reproach him. But he spun round, and seeing the disciples there, he took Peter to task, saying, 'Get behind me, Satan: for you are preoccupied not with the things of God, but with the things of man.'

Reflection

The moment when Peter confessed his faith in Christ tends to be portrayed as one of the most momentous events in the Gospel narratives – a supreme moment of understanding and a corresponding expression of commitment. To me, though, it is also an enigmatic moment; as much a day Peter would have wanted to forget as remember. Certainly, he declared Jesus to be the Messiah, but was he alone in this perception or simply voicing the opinion held by his fellow apostles? The idea that he understood who Jesus was more clearly than they did is given the lie in what follows, when far from being the rock of the Church, as he is described in other accounts of this incident, he is labelled 'Satan'. Strong stuff indeed!

Perhaps the greatest lesson we can draw from this story is that coming to faith is not the one-off event we sometimes imagine but an ongoing process that never ends. Peter thought he had understood the nature of Christ, and, to a point, he had. He was to imagine the same again later, professing his undying loyalty, only to deny his faith shortly afterwards. Later still, he was to recognise that his distinction between Jew and Gentile, clean and unclean, had no place in the Christian message. Faith was never a finished article but always on the production line, being shaped, added to, refined, polished. Beware the one who thinks they've arrived and who believes they have fathomed the depths of the gospel. Avoid such an error yourself. We may know the truth but, in this life at least, we will never know the whole truth.

Prayer

Sovereign God,
    open my heart to all you have yet to say,
    yet to do
    and yet to teach.
Help me to recognise that, far from being over,
    my journey has only just begun;
    that however far I may have come,
    there is always more to see,
    more to learn
    and more to understand.
Amen.

113
1 Corinthians 3:2, 3a
Tuck in

Because you were unready for solid food, I fed you instead with milk, which was all you seemed able to stomach. And because, even now, you remain preoccupied with the flesh, you are still not ready.

Reflection

Rumour has it that a fast-food store is to open in the town where I live. It's hard to believe, for the town centre there has been struggling for some time. Like so many places, it's become inundated with charity shops while other traders struggle to get by. The proposed new outlet, however, might just possibly prosper, given the public's seemingly insatiable appetite for convenience food. Never mind that its nutritional value is questionable, that much of it may actually do us more harm than good – most people seem to be happy so long as its tasty, cheap and cheerful. A hamburger and chips, it appears, washed down by a bottle of Coke, will typically do very nicely.

When it comes to spiritual sustenance, we, like the Corinthians to whom Paul was writing, can be equally careless. Instead of hungering and thirsting after righteousness, we feed ourselves on what has little, if any, power to satisfy, at best nibbling the occasional scrap of what is able to nourish the soul. We neglect the living bread and water offered by Christ, intent rather on consuming as much as possible of what this world has to offer. When did we last spend quality time studying an unfamiliar passage of Scripture, reflecting on matters of faith, or communing with God in prayer? When did we last seek true spiritual nourishment? Many of the Corinthians, it seems, never moved on from baby food to something more solid. What about us?

Prayer

Loving God,
>too often I forget to nourish myself spiritually,
>assuming I can go for days,
>even weeks,
>without doing anything to meet that hunger deep within.

I turn my back on food that satisfies,
>cramming my life instead with what leaves me spiritually debilitated,
>a mere child in faith.

Forgive my misplaced priorities,
>and teach me to hunger and thirst instead after righteous,
>for bread of life and living water that will help me to grow towards maturity in Christ.

Amen.

114
1 Corinthians 13:11
Growing up

When I was young, I spoke, thought and reasoned like a child, but once I became an adult I put aside such childish ways.

Reflection

The children raced around the toyshop in a state of high excitement, picking up first this, then that, eager to buy just about everything in sight. Their parents, though, were clearly less enthusiastic, and with good reason, for they knew full well that should they succumb to their children's pleas their home would soon be littered with discarded toys. As we get older we learn the value of money and how easy it is to fritter it away, but most of us in our childhood days would have been equally entranced by that toyshop's wares.

We grow up and out of things not just in life but also in faith – or at least we should do. We start off knowing just a little of God and grasping a mere fraction of what commitment means or the issues it throws up, our allegiance partial to say the least. Signs of Christ-like qualities in our lives are few and far between, for we are still fledglings, infants in discipleship. Yet if we are serious about our commitment, our faith will grow and mature, and our understanding will deepen as time goes by. It doesn't happen by itself though, any more than a child without schooling will reach their potential. We need to be open to the guidance of God's Spirit, eager to learn and ready to work at our faith. Do that and, like Paul, we will give up childish things and move a little closer to knowing God, even as we are fully known.

Prayer

Almighty God,
    instead of being seriously committed to you,
    I play at discipleship,
    rarely stretching my horizons or responding to your challenge.
Give me a real desire to move forward,
    to make progress in my journey of discovery.
Teach me to be childlike in attitude,
    but not childish;
    to display the hunger of youth to learn and experience more,
    so that I may acquire true wisdom –
    a living knowledge of you.
Amen.

Ephesians 4:11-14a, 15

Pot-bound Christians

He gave some to be apostles, some prophets, some evangelists, and some pastors and teachers, to prepare God's people for practical service and to build up the body of Christ until we are united in faith and the knowledge of the Son of God, attaining maturity corresponding to the full measure we see in Christ. Then we will no longer be like children. Instead, speaking the truth in love, we will in every respect grow into the one who is the Head; that is, Christ.

Reflection

I couldn't work it out at all. It has been doing well until then – a beautiful healthy plant growing with seemingly inexhaustible vigour – but now something was wrong; the once glossy leaves a listless yellow, new growth sparse and the stems spindly. I tried feeding, watering, pruning it, but to no avail – the malaise continued to worsen. Then, suddenly, I realised the problem, a tangle of roots protruding from the base of the container providing the vital clue. The plant was pot-bound, crying out for space in which to spread its feet. A few weeks later, re-potted with a liberal supply of fresh compost, it was romping away with all its former exuberance.

The analogy with faith is clear enough. When we start out in discipleship growth is rapid, everything new and exciting, so much to learn and discover – our commitment seeming to blossom with every passing day. Imperceptibly, however, the process stutters, slows, stops, until, instead of growing in faith, our devotion starts to shrivel and our enthusiasm to fade. We become comfortably ensconced in the same old soil, resenting any disturbance, unaware that our faith is being starved and suffocated, inexorably sucked dry. If it is not ultimately to die, we need to be open to new horizons, receptive to ideas other than our own, and ready to explore new avenues of service. You may have grown once, you may think you are growing still, but the reality may be that you've become a pot-bound Christian. The more vehemently you reject that possibility, the more likely it may be.

Prayer

Living God,
    you have sown the seed of faith within me,
    but I have prevented it from growing as it should.
My commitment starts to flag and my vision to wilt,
    cramped by the narrowness of my horizons,
    suffocated by complacency
    and starved of resources to help it flourish.
Forgive me for accepting that as the norm.
Help me to open my life to you
    so that you can feed me through your word,
    nourish me through your Spirit
    and nurture me through Christ.
Amen.

116
Jude v. 20

Build yourselves up

You then, dear friends, must continue to build yourselves up in your most sacred faith, praying through the Holy Spirit.

Reflection

When I was in hospital a while back, undergoing a course of high-dose chemotherapy, I didn't fancy eating much. In fact, it got to a point when I didn't fancy eating *at all*; even the *thought* of food turned my stomach. For a few days, I was almost wholly dependent on *Complan*, a liquid food explicitly created to help build people up. I can't say that I particularly enjoyed it, but in the circumstances it was just the thing, helping to give me the strength I needed when I needed it most.

It's important to build ourselves up spiritually as well as physically, and far better to make a daily habit of doing so rather than only remembering its importance in times of crisis. Yet we so often fail to make time for God – neglectful of his word, inconstant in prayer, careless in fellowship, forgetful of his love – and our discipleship consequently fades away, becoming a shadow of what it used to be. To change the metaphor, instead of daily building up our faith, placing fresh bricks on top of old, we allow it to crumble and fall into disrepair. Don't let that happen to you. 'Build yourselves up in your most sacred faith' before its health is weakened or altogether undermined.

Prayer

Loving God,
> for all my talk of commitment I'm careless in discipleship,
> cavalier about my relationship with you.

I pray intermittently,
> too often as an afterthought rather than as my first impulse.

I'm cursory in my reading of the Scriptures,
> doing so as much out of habit or duty
> as with any real expectation of you speaking to me.

I fail often even to consider you,
> my thoughts all for myself and the things of this world.

Forgive me,
> and help me to build up my faith so that it may truly become strong,
> able to meet whatever life may throw against it and still stand firm.

Amen.

THE TRANSFIGURATION

117

Mark 9:2-4

A glimpse of glory

Six days after this, Jesus took Peter, James and John up on to a lofty mountain with him, where they were alone together, removed from all, and there Jesus was transfigured before them. His garments gleamed a dazzling white, such as no fuller on earth could ever whiten them; and alongside Jesus, in conversation with him, appeared Moses and Elijah.

Reflection

I've never found the story of the Transfiguration an easy one to understand. It calls to mind the words in *Alice in Wonderland*: 'curiouser and curiouser', and is even vaguely suggestive of the claims of certain soap powders to wash whiter than white. Yet the strangeness of the incident should not blind us to its underlying message. This was no sensational sideshow designed to dispel doubts among the inner circle of disciples. On the contrary, it was a glimpse of the extraordinary in what had seemed an ordinary moment, a blossoming of faith leading to a deeper vision. At least that's how I read it. The three disciples are walking with Jesus, listening to his words, reflecting on his ministry, and, suddenly, it's not just a mountain they ascend but a spiritual peak – a high spot in which the reality of who Jesus is dawns on them. They discern, albeit fleetingly, that he is the fulfilment of the law and the prophets, represented by Moses and Elijah. They realise he is sent from God, dazzling in his splendour. They catch a brief vision of Christ in all his glory. Life would never be quite the same for them again, for this is the moment in which faith came of age, their old picture of Jesus exposed as hopelessly inadequate.

We can imagine, in our turn, that, having committed ourselves to Christ, we are well advanced along the path of faith, but we should never underestimate the power of Jesus to surprise us. The message here is similar to that of Peter's confession of Christ – namely that our knowledge of Jesus and our understanding of his glory will never be complete until this life is over and we meet him face to face. Until then, let us make time to be alone in his presence – to listen, hear and reflect – so that perhaps we too may glimpse a little more of his awesome wonder.

Prayer

Almighty God,
>forgive me for too often muddling along in life,
>>frustrating your will and quenching your Spirit through the narrowness of my vision.

Give me today a new sense of all you want to achieve
>and of the ways you are able to use me in accomplishing your purpose.

Stir my imagination
>and send me out renewed in faith
>>to live and work for your glory.

Amen.

118
Luke 9:29, 30, 32, 33
Letting go

As he prayed, his face was transformed and his clothes became a dazzling white. Then two men appeared, Moses and Elijah, talking with him. Peter and those who were with him, having fallen asleep, were startled into wakefulness and they saw his glory and the two men alongside him. As these two departed Peter said to Jesus, not really knowing what he was saying, 'Master, it is good for us to be here. Let us make three tents: one for you, one for Moses and one for Elijah.'

Reflection

Some moments mean so much to us that we wish we could pop them into a bottle and preserve them unchanged so that the happiness they bring never fades. I feel like that as I write, having spent a wonderful weekend with my family, away from it all – no work, no telephone, no pressures – an opportunity to unwind, spend some quality time with the children and rejoice in the indescribable beauty of this world God has given us. The memories of that time are still fresh in my mind as I sit now in my garden, the last rays of the sun dipping below the trees and a blackbird singing its heart out nearby. If I could put time on hold, I couldn't choose a better moment than this. Yet, if I could do that, how long would my joy remain untarnished? Unpalatable though it is to admit it, familiarity would soon rob the moment of its magic. In this world, life must move on if it is to keep its sparkle.

That was a truth Peter was to learn the hard way at that mysterious event we call the Transfiguration. He recognised the moment as special and wanted to keep hold of it, to the point of suggesting that he and his colleagues build tents so that Jesus, Moses and Elijah could remain there a little longer. It wasn't to be, though. Life had to move on. Jesus had to walk the way of the cross for which he had been born; Peter and his fellow apostles had more to learn, more to experience and more to understand.

The lesson holds true for us today. One day we will savour a joy that will never fade or end but, until then, we must treasure every God-given moment for what it is and then move on. We cannot preserve any moment, no matter how special. Attempt to do so and far from holding on to it, we will destroy it instead.

Prayer

Loving God,
    save me from so dwelling on what has been
    that I overlook your blessings now
    and your promise of joy to come.
Open my heart to new experiences of your love
    and new insights into your greatness,
    so that I may know you better each day,
    until that time I rejoice in your presence for all eternity.
Amen.

HOLY WEEK

Palm Sunday

119

Mark 11:7-10

A royal welcome

After they had brought the colt to Jesus and spread their cloaks over it, he sat on it. Many among the crowd spread their cloaks out on the road, while others cut down branches from the fields and spread those likewise. Those in the vanguard of the procession and those bringing up the rear cried out, 'Hosanna! Blessed is the one who comes in the Lord's name! Blessed is the coming kingdom of our forefather David! Hosanna in the highest heaven!'

Reflection

Coming in with a bang, going out with a whimper – in the eyes of many that could be said to describe the last days of the life of Jesus leading up to the cross. One moment he was accorded a positively rapturous welcome as he rode into Jerusalem, and the next they were baying for his blood, declaring that they had no other king but Caesar. It's a truly breathtaking turnaround in his fortunes, and a reader coming to the story for the first time could be forgiven for thinking that those who greeted Jesus as their king on Palm Sunday were sadly mistaken – misguided if not deluded. To a point they'd be right, for any hopes they may have had that Jesus was intending to stage some kind of political coup in order to establish an earthly kingdom were to be thoroughly quashed in the week ahead. But it was precisely through all that followed – the mocking and flogging, the crown of thorns, the agony of the cross – that he took up his throne, opening the way to a kingdom beyond this world.

The betrayal, arrest and crucifixion of Christ were not some unfortunate error that was somehow rectified at Easter, but the fulfilment of God's purpose: Jesus established his rule through surrendering his all. That is the Lord we worship – the one who came to serve rather than conquer, to bring life through enduring death. That is the Saviour we seek to honour. If we see him as sovereign yet not as servant, as raised high without also being brought low, then we, too, like so many who welcomed him on that first Palm Sunday, will have altogether missed the point.

Prayer

Lord Jesus Christ,
    save me from confusing the values of this world with your own,
    from seeing your heavenly rule as one that forces itself on
    people –
    demanding,
    coercing,
    imposing.
Teach me that, instead, yours is the way of love;
    one that invites a response –
    surrender,
    sacrifice,
    service.
Help me, then, to deny myself in order to discover who I really am;
    to be last so as to be first;
    to lose my life in order to find it –
    to walk the royal way of the cross.
Amen.

120
Luke 19:36-42

Changing our tune

As he rode, people carpeted the road with their cloaks. Then, as he started the descent from the Mount of Olives, the whole multitude of the disciples began loudly and joyfully to praise God for the mighty deeds they had seen, saying, 'Blessed is the king who comes in the name of the Lord! Peace in heaven, glory in the highest heaven!' Some Pharisees in the crowd said to him, 'Teacher, rebuke your disciples and tell them to stop.' He answered, 'I tell you this, if they were to keep silent, the very stones would shout out.' As he caught sight of the city, he wept over it, saying, 'If only you recognised this day the things that make for peace! Instead, though, they are hidden from your eyes!'

Reflection

It was only a children's story but it made the point well. 'Who will help me sow my seed?' asks the chicken. 'Not I', comes the answer. 'Who will help me reap the harvest?' 'Not I', comes the answer again. 'Who will help me grind the flour? Knead the dough? Bake the loaf? 'Not I . . . not I . . . not I.' Then, finally, the all-important question: 'Who will help me eat the bread?' and, immediately, a change of tone: 'Me! Me! Me!' It is an illustration, of course, of the fickleness of human nature, our friendship and loyalty so often depending on what's in it for us.

So it was on that first Palm Sunday as Jesus entered Jerusalem to the acclaim of the crowds. 'Who will welcome me as king?' his actions seemed to be saying, and the answer was 'Me!' Who wants to share in the kingdom of God?' and again the answer is 'Me!' Yet, just a few days later when the crunch question comes – 'Who will follow the way of the cross?' – the response from many is so very different: 'Not I!' – or, to put it more accurately, 'We have no king but Caesar. Crucify! Crucify! Crucify!' Palm Sunday is a day that challenges us concerning our loyalty, asking how ready we are to follow when faith is demanding and the going gets tough. Thank God, it is also about the one who, however often we may change our tune, stays faithful to us to the point of death.

Prayer

Lord Jesus Christ,
> so often my commitment is short-lived, superficial and self-centred,
> more about *my* well-being than *your* kingdom.

Thank you that though I am faithful to you in so little,
> you are faithful in so much;
> that though I repeatedly change my tune,
> your love never fails.

Forgive my weakness and, by your grace,
> help me to offer you true allegiance,
> whatever you may ask,
> to the glory of your name.

Amen.

Holy Monday to Wednesday

121

Mark 10:32

One step beyond

They were on the road leading to Jerusalem. Jesus was walking ahead of them, and they were amazed for, as they followed, they were afraid. He took the twelve aside once again, and began to tell them what was going to happen to him.

Reflection

What would you do if someone told you to lie on a bed of nails, walk across hot coals, bungee-jump off the Severn Bridge or parachute off the Empire State Building? If you've any sense, you wouldn't do it – I know *I* wouldn't! But how about if the person who posed those challenges promised to do each of them first, so that you could watch and learn from their experience, assured that each could be done before you followed suit? Well, I still wouldn't be convinced, but it's just possible that some of you bolder souls out there might have a try! When someone is willing to lead the way it makes a big difference, giving some people at least the courage they might not otherwise have had.

That willingness to take the lead characterised the life and ministry of Christ. It's there in our reading, Jesus knowing that his journey to Jerusalem was going to lead to his death, yet, far from holding back, dragging his feet or making an excuse to go no further, we see him leading the way, one step ahead of his disciples. We see it again following his resurrection, women going to the tomb to anoint his body, only to be told, 'He is not here. He has been raised from the dead and has gone ahead of you to Galilee. There you will see him' (Matthew 28:6a, 7b). The message holds for whatever we may face. Whether it be a time of testing or blessing, darkness or light, tears or laughter, we can be sure that Jesus is with us; not simply by our side but leading the way, one step beyond.

Prayer

Lord Jesus Christ,
    teach me that, whatever I may face, you will guide my footsteps,
    showing me the path I must take
    and ensuring that nothing can ever separate me from
    your presence.
Send me back, then, to my journey of discipleship
    redeemed in love,
    renewed in faith,
    restored in strength
    and refreshed in spirit.
Amen.

122
Mark 11:15

Totally devoted to you!

Then they arrived at Jerusalem.

Reflection

Some years ago, there was a song in the charts from the hit musical *Grease* with the title 'Hopelessly devoted to you'. It was a song about love – a love sufficiently strong to overcome hurt and rejection in order to establish a lasting relationship. There is a sense, though on a far deeper level, in which that title perfectly sums up the attitude of Jesus towards the whole of humankind, nowhere exhibited more clearly than in the week leading up to the cross.

We see it, believe it or not, in those five simple words of our reading. They look simple enough, don't they? But beneath the surface they bear eloquent testimony to the awesome love of Christ, for, humanly speaking, Jerusalem was the last place Jesus should have been heading for. The knives were out for him, his enemies determined finally to silence him, and Jesus knew it as well as anyone. Yet he carried on, setting his face towards Jerusalem, refusing to be deflected from his path. He went willingly to his death, despite all it cost him – despite the emotional, physical and spiritual trauma he endured, just like any other human being. Why? Quite simply, because he loves us, his devotion to us greater than any we might show to him. That song title could have been written about Jesus, except for one thing; his love wasn't hopeless – anything but – it brought hope, joy and life to all. What we see in Christ is something more wonderful still: the one who is totally devoted to you!

Prayer

Lord Jesus Christ,
> I am reminded today that you didn't just accept death for my sake
> but you chose it;
> that you didn't simply let things happen
> but planned them in advance,
> knowing the way you would take,
> down to that final agony on the cross.

You staked all,
> you gave all,
> and you did so willingly for the sake of people like me.

Such love is too wonderful to comprehend,
> but I thank you for it with all my heart,
> and offer you my joyful praise in glad response.

Amen.

123
Luke 9:23, 24
Taking up our cross

He said to them all, 'If any want to come after me, let them deny themselves and take up their cross daily, and then follow me. For those wishing to save their life will lose it, but those who lose their life for my sake will save it.'

Reflection

A row hit the headlines a while back concerning the right of people to wear a crucifix at their place of work. For some it represents a fundamental human and religious right; for others, the practice is potentially intrusive and divisive. Ironically, many who wear a crucifix profess no Christian faith whatsoever, using it purely for ornamentation rather than to make any kind of statement. And though, as Christians, we may justifiably feel that a simple crucifix offers a discreet way of professing our allegiance, we should beware of focusing too much on the outward symbol. Taking up our cross involves far more than displaying it on our person. It embraces the whole person and every aspect of life, entailing a willingness to put God and others first and self last.

That's what we see in Jesus, and especially so in the week leading up to his death. He knew what was in store for him – the agony, humiliation and darkness that lay ahead – and he knew that those he would do it for would betray, deny and abandon him, yet he continued regardless, offering his all for their sake and for ours. He was taking up his cross, literally, and carrying it to the place of execution where he was to deny himself in the most costly way possible.

Holy Week calls us not to outer show but to inner commitment, to a life consecrated to his service, a discipleship that is willing to make sacrifices and surrender itself to God's will. The right to wear a crucifix may be an important one, but what matters most of all is whether we're prepared actually to take up our cross and follow in the footsteps of Christ.

Prayer

Lord Jesus Christ,
   save me from a faith that is little more than a veneer.
Teach me to wear the cross not simply as an ornament
   but in my heart,
   to take it up inside as well as outside,
   consecrating more of my life more completely to you.
Amen.

124
Luke 22:8-13
Unsung disciples

Jesus sent Peter and John, with the words, 'Go and make ready the Passover meal so that we might share it together.' They replied, 'Where would you like us to prepare it?' 'Listen,' he answered, 'the moment you enter the city you'll be met by a man carrying a water jar. Follow him into the house he enters and say to the one who owns the house, "The teacher asks, 'Where is the room in which I can share Passover with my disciples?'" He'll lead you to a spacious furnished room upstairs. Get things ready there.' They did as he asked, and everything worked out just as he had predicted; so they prepared the Passover celebration.

Reflection

'First, I'd like to thank my wife and family for their faithful support; then, there's my manager, my agent, my friends . . .' We've all heard speeches like that, haven't we? Whether it's an Oscar winner, a sports personality having just won a prestigious event, an author awarded the Booker prize, or any other celebrity achieving recognition in their chosen field, the routine is much the same. And why not, for each of us, famous or otherwise, have people to whom we owe much; those who have helped make things possible. The speeches may often be boring, even embarrassing to listen to, but they nonetheless give well-deserved thanks to those behind the scenes.

There are no such speeches associated with Jesus in the days leading up to the cross, but there are hints of at least two people who played such an incognito role. The first was the owner of the colt upon which Jesus rode into Jerusalem. It only needed the disciples to say, 'The Lord needs it', for him gladly to let it go. The second was the owner of the upper room in which Jesus and the apostles shared the Last Supper. Again, we have no idea who he was, but he also played his part in God's purpose through allowing Jesus to use his room in this way. These two shadowy individuals remind us that we can offer service in simple, practical ways that are no less valuable than 'spiritual' contributions. Our gifts may not be those that catch the eye, and it may be that we prefer it that way, but that does not mean we have nothing to offer. All of us have a part to play in God's kingdom and all have something to contribute in the service of Christ.

Prayer

Lord,
    you do not call me to a position of eye-catching responsibility
    in your service,
    but you teach me that I have a part to play nonetheless;
    that, whatever my gifts,
    I have a contribution to make to your purpose.
Teach me, then, to listen for your voice
    and, when you call, to respond gladly,
    offering whatever you ask whenever you need it,
    not for any recognition I may receive
    but for the joy of contributing to your kingdom.
Amen.

125
1 Corinthians 1:18, 23, 24
Conveying what message?

The message of the cross to those who are perishing is folly, but to us who are being saved it is the mightiness of God. We proclaim Christ crucified, an offence to the Jews and plain folly to others, but to those who have been called, whether Jews or Greeks, it is the message of Christ, the power and wisdom of God.

Reflection

A society to which I belong spent many months recently debating the adoption of a new logo. They were concerned that their old one sent out the wrong message, anchoring them in the past rather than future, so they invested considerable time, not to mention money, in commissioning a new one. Are logos really that important? You have only to consider the millions of pounds that large companies splash out on them to realise that they are. A catchy design can capture the public's imagination, fixing a business firmly in the marketplace and establishing an image in the mind's eye of everything it's associated with.

As Christians we don't have a logo as such, but if there's one thing people think of in relation to the Church it's surely a cross. We see it on church buildings, on Bibles and hymnbooks, on banners, signs and posters, or worn round the neck as a crucifix, and many across the world still make the sign of the cross upon themselves, whether out of faith or superstition. But what image does the cross conjure up in people's minds? We may like think it speaks to people of Christ crucified, but the reality is this: the average person today, with little if any knowledge of the Christian faith, will judge the cross and indeed the Church itself by those who claim to represent it: by people like you and me. We need to live in such a way, then, that its true message comes across: the message of God's love in Christ, so passionate and intense that he gave everything to make it known. That's what the cross should speak of, what the Church should speak of, and for that to happen it's what your life must speak of too.

Prayer

Gracious God,
    save me from conveying the wrong message,
    from putting across a negative or false picture of the gospel.
Though I wear no badge, Lord,
    no label,
    help me so to know you that everything I am speaks of your love for all,
    witnessing in a way that words alone can never achieve
    to the awesome extent of your grace.
Amen.

MAUNDY THURSDAY

126

Matthew 26:21, 22

Constant to the end

While they were eating, he said to them, 'Mark what I'm telling you. One of you is going to betray me. At his words they were filled with sorrow and responded, one after the other, 'Surely you can't be referring to me, Lord?'

Reflection

A week, they say, is a long time in politics. Today's hero can become tomorrow's villain; a lead in the polls can turn to a lead for the opposition upon the announcement of poor economic or unemployment figures; a seemingly blossoming political career can be snuffed out through press revelations of a skeleton in the cupboard. A week, equally, proved to be a long time in the life and ministry of Jesus, exhibiting an apparently similar change in fortunes – seven days that we've come to know as Holy Week.

On the one hand, it highlights human faithlessness writ large. There's Judas Iscariot, betraying his friend Jesus in the garden of Gethsemane with a kiss. There's Simon Peter who, just as Jesus had predicted, denies all knowledge of the man who, just a short time before, he'd proclaimed his readiness to die for. There are the remaining apostles who melt into the shadows when the heat is on. And, of course, there are the crowds who, having welcomed him so volubly as he rode into Jerusalem, now vociferously demand his death. It's a sorry picture of human faithlessness and fickleness. Yet, of course, Holy Week speaks also of incomparable faith*ful*ness – the passionate commitment of Christ not just to his disciples but to all who would follow him then, now and beyond, despite the feeble faith and callow commitment we may show. It speaks of the one who, in Paul's words, 'died for us while we were yet sinners' (Romans 5:8), who gave everything despite knowing the worst of us. If this day reminds us more than any other of how fickle we can be, it proclaims also the constancy of God's love, come what may!

Prayer

Saviour Christ,
> I am reminded today of how one of your disciples betrayed you . . .
> and of how I betray you in turn;
> of how one of your closest friends denied you . . .
> and of how I deny you also;
> of how your chosen followers abandoned you . . .
> and of how I sometimes do the same.

Thank you for the knowledge that though I constantly fail,
> you will not fail to stay constant.

Amen.

127
Matthew 26:28, 29

Giving blood

'This is my blood of the covenant, poured out for many to bring forgiveness from sins. I tell you the truth, I will not drink of the fruit of the vine again until that day when I drink it new with you in my Father's kingdom.'

Reflection

Do you regularly give blood? Some can't for medical reasons, but if all that's stopping you is a squeamishness about needles, or simply laziness, maybe it's time to think again. I resumed giving some years back, having chickened out of doing so for a considerable time previously, and though I can't say I enjoyed the experience I was keenly aware of the importance of donations. Any possibility of my forgetting to donate was countered by regular bulletins that are sent out to donors, each full of facts, figures and heart-warming stories detailing how blood transfusions can change people's lives – indeed, often meaning the difference between life and death itself. But for my unexpected illness, I would still be donating now.

At the heart of the gospel is the giving of blood in a different sense – the blood shed by Jesus on the cross. It wasn't just a bagful, gently extracted and followed by a refreshing cup of tea; it was his lifeblood, freely offered for the life of the world; a sacrifice involving physical, emotional and spiritual cost. Yet it was gladly surrendered to transform human lives, making the difference not just between life and death but between life and *life eternal*. Rejoice then, today, in what God, through Christ, has so wonderfully given, for you, for me and for all.

Prayer

Lord Jesus Christ,
    thank you for giving your blood,
    your all,
    to bring life to the world.
Remind me that you drank of the cup of suffering not for yourself
    but for others,
    that cup representing the greatest of gifts,
    precious beyond words.
Whenever I drink,
    remind me that you are the true vine offering life-giving wine,
    now and in your Father's kingdom.
Help me to celebrate that awesome truth,
    this and every day.
Amen.

128
Mark 14:22-25
Look both ways

During supper, he took bread, and having given thanks he broke it and gave it to them, saying, 'Take this; it is my body.' Then he took a cup, and, giving thanks to God, he handed it to them; and they all drank from it. Then he said, 'This is my blood, the blood of the covenant, shed for many. I tell you the truth, I will not drink of the fruit of the vine again until that day when I drink it new with you in the kingdom of God.'

Reflection

There's a piece of advice we will all have received many times as children: 'Look both ways.' I refer, of course, to learning to cross the road, and to the advice of the Green Cross Code: 'Look right, look left, look right again.'

There is a sense in which Maundy Thursday invites us to do something very similar, only this time we are talking not about left and right but about the past and the future, and the difference those make to the present. 'Take this; it is my body,' said Jesus, and, as Paul reminds us in his letter to the Corinthians, these words are to serve as a constant reminder to Christians, calling to mind his suffering and death. Yet it was not all solemnity, for there was also a message of hope; a hint of joy to come in his words, 'I will not drink of the fruit of the vine again until that day when I drink it new with you in the kingdom of God.' Here, then, is a call to look backwards and forwards, to remember and to anticipate. It is a message not just for Maundy Thursday, nor simply for each time we break bread and share wine, but for each day and every moment. We are called to live here and now in the light of what God has done and what he promises to do.

Prayer

Lord Jesus Christ,
> I remember today everything you did to bring me life:
> the heartbreak you experienced,
> the fear you faced,
> the questions you wrestled with
> and the agony you endured.

I look forward today to what you have promised:
> a time when I will share with you in your Father's kingdom
> and there there will be an end to sorrow and suffering,
> sin and death.

Teach me to look back,
> to look forwards,
> and thus to commit myself in confidence to your service here and now,
> knowing that you are the same Lord,
> yesterday,
> today
> and tomorrow.

Amen.

129
Mark 14:32-36
The valley of tears

After this, they went to a spot called Gethsemane. 'Sit here while I pray,' Jesus instructed his disciples. Taking Peter, James and John with him a little further, he suddenly became distraught. 'I am so crushed by grief that it's killing me,' he told them. 'Remain here and keep a lookout.' Going on a few steps more by himself, he prostrated himself before God, asking to be spared his coming hour if it was in any way possible. 'Abba, Father,' he pleaded, 'nothing is beyond you, so take this cup away from me. Yet don't do what I want; do what you have to do.'

Reflection

'I shouldn't be feeling like this. I know it's wrong but I just can't help it.' I've lost count of the times I've heard comments like that from people feeling guilty about being depressed or miserable. The idea that they've anything to be ashamed of is ridiculous, of course, yet there are subtle pressures in the Church today that can make us feel we should banish all negative thoughts from our minds. Much modern worship focuses upon themes such as joy, praise and celebration, to the exclusion of other emotions, and this emphasis seems to be reinforced by verses like Philippians 4:4, which states: 'Rejoice in the Lord always; again I say it: rejoice!' If we're not careful, the sorrowful and downhearted can feel excluded, even to the point of regarding their feelings as a sin. They feel that they should somehow be able to rise above sorrow; that, even though they are not immune from tragedy, it shouldn't hit them in quite the same way that it does non-believers.

That is one reason why the story of Gethsemane is so important, for here we see God identifying himself with human sorrow. 'My heart is ready to break with grief,' said Jesus; as the

New International Version puts it, 'My soul is overwhelmed with sorrow to the point of death.' Here is a reminder that God himself, through Christ, has shared in our blackest, bleakest moments. He is a God who not only understands what grief and heartbreak mean but also empathises with those experiencing them. Above all, he is a God who stays close to us through such times and who, finally, will bring hope after despair, laughter after tears and joy after sorrow.

Prayer

Loving God,
> I remember today all who mourn,
> their hearts broken by tragedy,
> tears a constant companion,
> laughter and happiness seeming a distant memory.

Reach out into their pain, heartache and sadness,
> and give them the knowledge that you understand their pain
> and share their sorrow.

May your arms enfold them,
> your love bring comfort,
> and your light finally scatter the shadows,
> so that they may know joy once more
> and celebrate life in all its fullness.

Amen.

130
Mark 14:51, 52

A changed life?

A certain young man accompanied him, wearing nothing but a linen cloth. They grabbed hold of him, but he wriggled out of the cloth and ran off naked.

Reflection

Who was the young man who ran off naked into the night at the time of the arrest of Jesus? That question has fascinated scholars across the years and although no definitive answer has been given, the general consensus of opinion favours John Mark, the writer of the Gospel in which this enigmatic character is mentioned. It's an intriguing thought, isn't it – both heart-warming and inspiring to think that someone so desperate to disassociate himself from Jesus could, in the space of a few years, become the writer of what most regard as the earliest of all the Gospels, eagerly testifying to his faith in the risen Christ.

If the conjecture is right, was this, I wonder, the first time that Mark had faced up to the incident? Presumably so, for why else refer to it so obliquely? It seems he still couldn't bring himself to come clean completely, yet he wanted to testify to what for him must have been the most marvellous truth in the already unforgettable gospel message: the fact that Jesus had changed *him*, turning his life inside out and upside down. The same testimony, together with a similar sense of wonder, can equally be ours! No one is outside the transforming power of his saving love and no mistake is beyond his forgiveness. He is constantly at work in the lives of all who will receive him, to redeem, renew and restore. Whoever you are, Jesus can change you!

Prayer

Loving God,
> you repeatedly show how you are able to change lives,
> not just forgiving past mistakes but also making people new,
> renewing them from within through your Holy Spirit.

Help me, then, to acknowledge all the feelings of guilt and shame that hold me down,
> and to open my life to your renewing touch in Christ.

Amen.

131
John 13:6-9, 12, 14-16
Ready to serve

He reached Simon Peter, who asked, 'Lord, do you intend to wash my feet?' Jesus replied, 'You don't understand what I am doing at the moment, but you will eventually.' 'No,' Peter retorted, 'you will never wash my feet!' Jesus answered, 'If I don't wash you, you cannot be part of me.' Hearing this, Peter burst out, 'Then not only my feet, Lord, but my hands and head as well!' After washing their feet, Jesus put on his robe, went back to the table and said to them, 'Do you understand the meaning of what I have just done? If I, your Lord and master, have washed your feet, you also ought to wash each other's feet. I have set an example for you to follow, so that you might do to others what I have done to you. I tell you this: servants are not greater than their master, nor are those who carry messages greater than the one who sent them.'

Reflection

'For yours is the power and the glory, for ever and ever. Amen.' So we repeat day after day, week after week, in the words of the Lord's Prayer. But what sort of power and glory are we talking about? Jesus' washing of his disciples' feet suggests that these terms should be understood somewhat differently from the way we typically interpret them, for his actions were a demonstration of service and humility, of putting self second and others first. Instead of issuing a rallying cry to his followers – a call to arms – Jesus stooped to perform the most menial of tasks; instead of declaring himself king, he assumed the role of a servant. This, said Jesus, is what his way involves, and this is the path that those who would follow him must take in turn. If we would exalt his name we must humble ourselves; if we would serve him we must serve others.

So what does that mean in practice? There's no single answer, for there are all kinds of ways we can put others before ourselves. It may be through serving as a carer or nursing a loved one. It may be through helping those who are incapacitated in some way. It may be through some form of service to the local community. Or it may simply be through putting another person's interests before our own. That's what Jesus asks of us: a readiness to deny ourselves for the good of others, a love and humility that is willing to see beyond looking after number one. How far do we honour that call?

Prayer

Loving God,
   I talk of service
   but am forgetful of others,
   speak of sacrifice
   but shy away from the prospect of costly commitment.
Teach me your way of humility,
   of truly putting others first,
   and help me in whatever way I can to do precisely that.
Amen.

132
John 13:36-38
All talk?

Simon Peter said to him, 'Lord, where are you going?' Jesus replied, 'You cannot follow me where I am going now, but you will some day.' Peter said, 'Lord, why can't I follow you now? I will lay down my very life for you.' 'Will you truly lay down your life for me,' Jesus responded. 'Mark my words: before the cock crows, you will renounce me three times.'

Reflection

'A penny off income tax, cheaper fuel, more investment in the health service and education, higher pensions, tough measures on crime . . . ' We've heard it all before, haven't we? The words trotted out by politicians every four years or so as the country braces itself for another election. It's not that the politicians set out to deceive us (well, not most of them, anyway); rather that, swept along on the tide of the moment, they find that when it comes to it, they simply can't deliver – their fine words exposed as all talk. So it was for Peter in the moments leading up to the cross. 'I will lay down my very life for you,' he declares, or, as Mark records his words, 'Even if I must die with you, I will never disown you.' Rash, impulsive words, no doubt, but he meant every word and fully believed he could honour such promises. Events, of course, were to prove him wrong. So what is the message here for us? That we, like Peter, are false and faithless? That we are often prone to empty rhetoric? Both are probably true. The key detail, however, is that Jesus knew full well that Peter would fail him, that his words were all talk, yet still he loved him – enough to continue to the cross, enough to have chosen him as the rock of his Church.

That's the wonder of this incident: that far from wanting him to punish himself afterwards for his failure, Jesus wanted Peter to know that he knew his weakness, understood he would fail, and yet still loved him. Here is the awesome message of the gospel – the message that gives hope to us all.

Prayer

Lord Jesus Christ,
> just as you chose ordinary human beings to be your followers
> during your ministry,
> so, I am reminded today, that you call me in turn.

Though I am as weak, foolish and fallible as any,
> still you love me;
> though I see so little good within me,
> you see someone worth dying for
> and worth sharing life with for all eternity.

For that awesome truth, thank you.
Amen.

GOOD FRIDAY

133

Matthew 26:69-75

A changed man

Peter sat outside in the courtyard, and a servant-girl approached him saying, 'You also were with Jesus the Galilean', but he denied it before them all, saying, 'I've no idea what you're talking about.' He went out to the porch, where another servant-girl saw him, and she said to those gathered there, 'This man was with Jesus of Nazareth.' He denied it once again, with an oath, 'I do not know the man.' Shortly afterwards, the bystanders came up and confronted Peter, 'There's no doubt that you also are one of them, for your accent gives you away.' Then he began to curse and swear, 'I do not know the man!' At precisely that moment, the cock crowed, and Peter remembered what Jesus had said: 'Before the cock crows, you will deny me three times.' He stumbled outside and wept bitterly.

Reflection

A few years ago my wife attended a reunion of former classmates. She found it a fascinating experience. A few had hardly altered but the majority had changed beyond recognition.

In our verses today, we encounter a man in whom there was to be a truly remarkable change. We meet him first as an ordinary fisherman going about his daily business, but following the call of Christ he quickly emerges as the leader of the apostles. All that, though, must have rung somewhat hollow on that awful night when, just as had been predicted, he denied Jesus three times.

Yet, when we turn to the book of Acts, what a different story we find. It is Peter, in Acts 2, who boldly speaks out for Christ on behalf of the apostles following the baptism of the Holy Spirit. Later, when his persistent testimony lands him in hot water with the authorities, he responds, 'Make up your own minds whether it is right in God's eyes to obey you rather than him. The fact is we cannot help but speak concerning everything we have seen and heard' (Acts 4:19, 20). From one afraid to be associated with Christ, Peter had changed to one proud to bear his name; from one whose only thought had been his own safety to one heedless of the cost of discipleship. Here is an astonishing testimony to the way Jesus is able to change lives. The change in us may not be quite so dramatic, but the message of Peter's story is clear: if Jesus could change his life, he can change anyone's!

Prayer

Lord Jesus Christ,
   remind me that as you changed Peter,
   so you can also change me;
   that you are constantly at work nurturing my faith,
   strengthening my commitment
   and deepening my experience of your love.
Take what I am and have been,
   and by your renewing, redeeming touch direct what I shall be,
   to the glory of your name.
Amen.

134
Mark 15:29-32a
A straight choice

The passers-by hurled insults at him, shaking their heads and saying, 'So, then, you who would destroy the temple and build it in three days: come down from the cross and save yourself!' The chief priests and teachers of the law joined in mocking him with similar taunts. 'He saved others,' they said, 'but he cannot save himself! Let this Messiah, the king of Israel, come down now from the cross, so that we might see and believe.'

Reflection

'Many a true word is spoken in jest.' So the saying has it, and if you need convincing of that, take a look at the taunts faced by Jesus on the cross. 'He saved others, but he cannot save himself!' – words of mockery and derision aimed at adding to the suffering already experienced by Jesus, and you can imagine his tormentors smirking, chuckling, congratulating themselves on their own wit. Make him eat his words, they thought; now let's see how smart he is!

Yet, if they had but known, they could not have spoken more profoundly, for those words give voice to the stark choice faced by Jesus and the love he showed in taking the path he did. Could he have saved himself? Of course he could. Not only could he have steered well clear of Jerusalem in the first place, but for someone who had healed the sick, stilled the storm, fed the multitude, even raised the dead, to come down from the cross was nothing, positively straightforward by comparison. Yet to do that would have been to go back on his mission and deny his calling; for it was only through his accepting suffering and death that he could open up the way to life for others. It was a straight choice, an 'either/or' rather than 'both/and' situation, and he chose to save us rather than himself.

'He saved others, but he cannot save himself.' How wrong they were, yet how right!

Prayer

Lord Jesus Christ,
> I remember today that you endured the humiliation
> of Gethsemane,
> the agony of the cross
> and the darkness of the tomb,
> not because you had to but because you chose to.

You could so easily have stepped down from the cross,
> but you didn't;
> you could have saved yourself,
> but you preferred instead to save the world.

However often I hear it,
> I am overwhelmed by the magnitude of your love
> and awesomeness of your sacrifice.

Receive my grateful praise and worship.
Amen.

135
Mark 15:34
The ultimate sacrifice

Then Jesus called out in a loud voice, 'Eloi, Eloi, lama sabachthani?' which translated means, 'My God, my God, why have you forsaken me?'

Reflection

Nothing takes us more powerfully and directly to the heart of this day than that desolate cry of Jesus from the cross: 'My God, my God, why have you abandoned me?' And no words, on the surface at least, could make it seem more inappropriately named, for what on earth can be good about Jesus feeling so helpless, so hopeless, so utterly bereft and alone? It's as though up to this point, despite everything he'd said, he'd been secretly hoping that God might somehow rescue him; that there might be a last-minute reprieve, a miraculous escape. Hadn't he, after all, cried out in Gethsemane, 'if it be possible, take this cup from me'? Was this, then, a crisis of faith as God failed to step into the breach?

It might seem that way, but the reality couldn't be more different. Yes, Jesus felt isolated, forsaken, and yes it was devastating beyond words, but this was what he had committed himself to doing right at the start of his ministry – not simply surrendering his life but taking upon himself the sins of the world, bearing them in his body, taking upon himself the punishment that should have been ours. There on the cross Jesus endured the agony of total separation from God, an agony not just of body but of spirit. Rather than abandon us, he faced what it means to feel utterly *abandoned*. In order to reconcile us with God, he was estranged. It was the ultimate sacrifice to make possible the ultimate gift: new life, resurrection life, lived for evermore. That's the message of Good Friday. Could any day be more *appropriately* named!

Prayer

Lord Jesus Christ,
    thank you for what you did on the cross
    and what you achieved through that sacrifice.
Thank you for accepting the punishment that was mine
    so that I might share the life that is yours.
For bringing me close to God through being made far from him,
    for reconciling me through being estranged,
    receive my grateful praise.
Amen.

136
Luke 23:44, 45a

God in the darkness

It was around midday, and darkness descended over the whole land until three o'clock in the afternoon, for the sun had ceased to shine.

Reflection

How many of us are scared of the dark? Probably few of us are afraid in the sense we once were as children, yet there is still something about darkness that makes us associate it with the sinister, evil and unknown. It is not surprising, then, that if there is one thing we associate with God and one symbol used for him more than any other, it is light. 'The Lord is my light and my salvation,' says Psalm 27; 'of whom shall I be afraid?' Or again, in Psalm 36, 'With you is the fountain of life; in your light we see light.'

So we could go on, piling one text on top of another. Yet, while all this is true, it is not the complete picture, and it's a good thing it isn't, for there are times when life seems dark, bleak, grim and forbidding; when even God seems far away such that we cry out in despair – times described by St John of the Cross as 'the dark night of the soul'. What do we make of moments like those? Has God no place in them? Must we face them alone? Not if the words of the Gospels concerning the death of Christ are to believed, for there we read of how darkness descended on the land as Jesus hung on the cross. It seemed, even to Jesus, as though God wasn't present but the reality, of course, was different. It was here that God was supremely and astonishingly at work, offering himself for the life of the world, paying the price that would set us free. Though darkness seemed to have overtaken the world, the reality was that the light of God's love was shining brighter than ever and nothing would be able to overcome it. There are times when, for the Christian as much as any other, life seems dark and God seems far away, but never feel that God has abandoned you, for sometimes it is in the darkest moments that he is there most of all.

Prayer

Living God,
    thank you that even when life seems dark and hopeless –
    when I search but cannot glimpse your presence
    and call yet cannot hear your voice –
    still you are with me,
    the light of your love continuing to shine,
    even though it's hidden.
May that knowledge sustain me through the bleakest moments,
    bringing the assurance that good will triumph over evil,
    hope replace despair,
    joy come after sorrow
    and life triumph over death –
    that even the deepest darkness will be turned to light.
Amen.

137
John 19:38-40

Secret disciples?

Joseph of Arimathea – a disciple of Jesus, albeit secretly because of his fear of the Jews – asked Pilate for permission to take away the body of Jesus. Pilate consented; so he went and removed the body. Nicodemus, who first came to Jesus by night, accompanied him, bringing with him a blend of myrrh and aloes, about a hundred pounds in weight. They took the body of Jesus and bound it, together with the spices, in linen cloths, following the burial custom of the Jews.

Reflection

Our first reaction, reading of Joseph of Arimathea and Nicodemus asking for the body of Jesus, is that it was too little, too late. A well-intentioned act, undoubtedly, but what use to Jesus was it now? If they'd stuck their necks out earlier, then how different things might have been. Yet is such an interpretation fair? Certainly open commitment from the start would have been better, but which of us would have acted differently in their place? To publicly declare allegiance to Jesus would have involved risk and, very likely, personal danger. For the ordinary people to follow him was bad enough in the eyes of the Jewish authorities; for a Pharisee it was unthinkable!

Many generations of Christians since have felt forced by persecution to be secret disciples: witness the catacombs of Rome or the story of Christians in the Soviet bloc before the demise of communism. For us, there is no such excuse. We have freedom of speech, freedom of conscience and freedom of belief. It's conceivable that we might suffer discrimination due to our faith but it's unlikely to be anything worse. Yet how many of us are up-front about our faith, proud to acknowledge it, ready to nail our colours firmly to the mast? Or, to put it another way, how many of those we regularly come into contact with have any inkling that we are Christians or any idea of what our faith means to us? At least Joseph and Nicodemus had some reason to be secretive. Have we?

Prayer

Lord Jesus Christ,
> instead of shining like a lamp in the world,
> too often I do the opposite,
> hiding my light under a bushel,
> even sometimes to the point of secret discipleship.

Forgive the feebleness of my commitment
> and weakness of my love,
> and help me to acknowledge you proudly as the light of my life,
> whatever the cost may be.

Amen.

138

Romans 5:6-8

Precious to him

When the time was right, Christ died for the ungodly in all their weakness. It is exceedingly rare for someone to die for anybody, even a righteous person, though perhaps if they're sufficiently good someone might actually dare to do so, but God proved his love for us in that while we were yet sinners, Christ died for us.

Reflection

I switched on the television today in readiness for the lunchtime news, and caught the tail end of a programme featuring an auction. Bidding was brisk at first and remained so for as long as the price was low, but as the price crept up so participation dwindled until finally there were two people left bidding against each other. They continued sparring for a time, each raising the price a little, but eventually it frightened one off, leaving the other victorious as the auctioneer's hammer dropped – 'Going, going, gone!' It was a decent price, but not as much as the seller had hoped for, not by a long way. A second item, though, fared even worse, failing to reach the reserve price and so being withdrawn from sale. Quite simply, no one valued it enough to match the vendor's valuation.

We, too, can feel undervalued, unappreciated, convinced that no one understands our true worth. And we're probably right. Most of us are wrapped up in our own little world, thinking of ourselves rather than others, too concerned with what they think of us to spare a thought for them. Most of us also are good at seeing faults in others that we fail to see in ourselves; quick to spot the worst and slow to discern the best. Little wonder then that the same is meted out to us. But with Jesus it's different. Even though compared to him we cannot begin to pass muster – we are all unworthy – he counts us of inestimable worth and values us enough to pay the ultimate price, giving his life to make us his, to redeem us from what denies and devalues life. Whoever you are, you matter to him. Others may dismiss you; he will not. You mean more to him than words can say.

Prayer
Gracious God,
    whenever we're tempted to undervalue ourselves,
    whenever we *are* undervalued,
    and whenever we fail to value others,
    remind us afresh of the lengths to which you went to make us yours,
    of the infinite worth you place on us all.
Amen.

EASTER EVE

139

Mark 15:43-47

Dealing with death

Joseph of Arimathea, a respected council member who was eagerly anticipating the dawn of God's kingdom, boldly approached Pilate and asked if he could take away Jesus' body. Uncertain whether Jesus was dead yet, Pilate summoned the centurion and asked whether and when he had died. On receiving confirmation from the centurion that Jesus was indeed dead, Pilate granted Joseph the body, whereupon Joseph bought a linen cloth, took down the body and used the cloth to shroud it before laying out the corpse in a tomb carved in the rock. Finally, he rolled a stone against the mouth of the tomb. Mary Magdalene and Mary, Joses' mother, saw for themselves where the body was laid.

Reflection

According to Sigmund Freud, it's impossible for us to imagine our own death. How true that is, I'm not sure, but – impossible or not – it's not something any of us *like* to contemplate. It's a spectre we thrust to the back of our minds and do our level best not to think about if at all possible. Death represents an enemy on so many levels, separating us from loved ones, extinguishing our hopes and dreams, relativising all our striving, plucking us rudely out of this world. And all that is not to mention the actual process of dying which, for many, is perhaps the most daunting prospect of all. No wonder talk of death continues to be a modern-day taboo, studiously and discreetly avoided. Yet, of course, death is one of the few things none of us can avoid. And that's why Holy Saturday, or Easter Eve, is important. Coming as it does between

Good Friday and Easter Sunday, it reminds us that God in Christ has shared not just our humanity, not just our life, but also our death.

That's what we remember today: that Jesus was cut down lifeless from the cross and sealed in a tomb. Rigor mortis would have set in, his body cold, inanimate, an empty shell. And for those who had known and loved him it was over, nothing left now other than to anoint his body one last time. Only, of course, that was not the final word. What appeared to be the end was in fact merely the beginning, as we will celebrate once more in the days ahead. But as well as rejoicing in God's gift of resurrection life, rejoice also in the knowledge that, however frightening it may seem, however bleak and hopeless, death can be faced with confidence, for God has been there too and will be with us in and through it.

Prayer

Living God,
    thank you for the awesome truth that, in Christ,
    you entered the darkness of death itself –
    the cold finality of the grave.
May that knowledge sustain and inspire me
    and all who wrestle with the prospect of death,
    together with those who mourn loved ones
    or face the prospect of bereavement.
Remind all that through experiencing death you have defeated it,
    not just once but for evermore,
    not just for Jesus
    but for us too.
Amen.

140

John 19:31-34a

He was dead

Since it was the day of preparation for the Passover, the Jews did not want dead bodies left on the cross during the Sabbath, especially because that Sabbath was a day of special import, so they asked Pilate to have the legs of those who had been crucified broken and their bodies removed. Accordingly, the soldiers broke the legs of the first and then the second of those crucified with Jesus, but when they came to Jesus, they saw he was already dead so they did not break his legs. Instead, one of the soldiers pierced his side with a spear.

Reflection

Some animals, when faced with danger, make use of a cunning trick. Instead of running or standing up to fight, they play dead, thus confusing their attacker, which is only interested in live prey. To hear some people talk, you might imagine that the crucifixion involved a similar trick. Maybe Jesus wasn't dead, after all, some suggest; perhaps in the coolness of the tomb he regained consciousness, and was subsequently whisked away by his followers under cover of darkness.

It's far-fetched, I know, but some people will believe anything rather than have their preconceptions challenged. The idea of resurrection simply goes against everything they believe about and experience in the world. Yet, one look at the Gospels – and at the Gospel of John in particular – leaves us in no doubt about the truth. Jesus was dead, a spear thrust into his side to make doubly certain. He was laid limp and lifeless in a tomb, and a stone rolled against the entrance. Humanly speaking it was over, the end of a wonderful ministry and an unforgettable man. He had shared our life; he had shared our death. If the story was to continue, it was out of human hands – it was down now to God.

Prayer

Lord Jesus Christ,
> I remember today that for those who saw life slip from you as you hung on the cross,
> there could be no mistaking the truth,
> no escaping the awfulness of the moment.

You endured the pain of betrayal,
> the hurt of denial,
> the humiliation of mockery
> and, finally, the awful isolation of separation from your Father as you took our sins on your shoulders –
> and you did it for such as me.

Lord Jesus,
> you gave so much;
> help me to give something back to you.

Amen.

EASTER

141
Matthew 27:62-66
The God who cannot be kept down

The following day – in other words, the day after that of preparation – the chief priests and the Pharisees congregated before Pilate and said, 'Your excellency, we recall how that deceiver said while he was alive, "After three days I will rise." Will you, then, order that the tomb be made secure until the third day? Otherwise his disciples may come and steal him away, and tell the people, "He has been raised from the dead" – a final deception that would be worse than the first.' Pilate said to them, 'You have a guard of soldiers; go and make it as secure as possible.' So they went and made the tomb secure by sealing it with a stone and leaving a guard in charge.

Reflection

When my daughter was a baby she had a wonderful inflatable toy called 'Bopper Bear'. No matter how hard or how often you knocked it over, it would always bounce back up again. I don't know if Kate enjoyed it, but I did!

There is something of that idea in the story of the resurrection, for we see there a supreme demonstration of the God who cannot be kept down. The enemies of Jesus had conspired together, determined finally to do away with him, and as they cut him limp and lifeless from the cross, sealing him in a tomb, they must have been convinced they had succeeded. Even then, they placed a guard outside the tomb, just to make sure. They were leaving nothing to chance. Yet, it didn't matter, for the next day what did they find but the stone rolled away and the tomb empty, their worst fears realised. How could it be? What could have happened? These are good questions, which anyone who disputes the resurrection still needs to answer. Hatred had done its worst, but the love of God could not be kept down. Christ was risen! It's as true today as ever; ultimately there is nothing and no one that can frustrate the will of God. Though many may still try and sometimes seem to succeed, ours is a God who will finally triumph, and who gives us the victory in turn.

Prayer

Living God,
    thank you for the great message at the heart of Easter:
    that your love could not be kept down,
    your purpose could not be defeated
    and your mercy could not be destroyed.
Teach me that what was true then is true now:
    that there is still nothing that can stand in the way of your
    sovereign power
    or your redeeming grace.
Assure me, then, however things may seem
    and even when faith seems to fly in the face of reason,
    to trust in you,
    confident that your will shall be done
    and your kingdom come.
Amen.

142
Matthew 28:11-14
The truth that couldn't be hidden

Some of the guards went into the city and told the chief priests what had happened. After the priests had called together the elders, they formulated a plan to give a generous bribe to the soldiers, telling them, 'You must say this, "His followers came during the night and made off with him while we were sleeping." If the governor gets to hear of this, we will reassure him and keep you out of trouble.' So the guards took the money and did as instructed.

Reflection

In 1972 a story hit the headlines in America that was to send shock waves across the world and lead to the unseating and disgrace of a president. It was, of course, the Watergate affair, a scandal that has gone down in history and forever tarnished the reputation of Richard M. Nixon. Had he made a clean breast of things at the start, he might just possibly have weathered the storm, bruised but intact, but instead he made the mistake of trying to conceal the truth through a veil of lies, half-truths and evasions. Presumably he seriously imagined this would work, that he would be able to dictate events and mould history to his wishes, but events were to prove him wrong.

So it was, likewise, for those who attempted to cover up the truth of the resurrection of Christ. They'd waited for years to get their man and had watched with a mixture of glee and relief as he was finally nailed to a cross and sealed in a tomb. At last, they thought, their problems were over, the impostor dealt with once and for all. And for a couple of nights they must have slept easy, congratulating themselves on their success. Imagine, then, their dismay when rumours began to circulate that he was alive after all; their incredulity when they went to the tomb to investigate for themselves and found no sign of the body. No wonder they tried to put a lid on it, to hush things up as best they could. But what they couldn't conceal were the changed lives and the witness of those who had experienced the reality of the risen Christ for themselves, the faith that burned within them, the love they showed and the joy they displayed. Together these pointed, and still point today, to a truth that they couldn't conceal; a truth that, despite their efforts, they couldn't kill off, for the simple but special reason that they couldn't kill off Jesus either!

Prayer

Loving God,
> thank you for the message of the empty tomb
> and of your appearing to your followers,
> and for the testimony of countless generations since
> who have met with and known Christ for themselves,
> his presence through his Spirit firing their faith
> and inspiring their commitment.

Thank you that their experience is mine too;
> that I also can testify to the reality of your resurrection
> not through what I have learnt or read
> but through your living presence within my heart.

Amen.

143
Matthew 28:15a

Truth will out!

So the guards took the money and did as instructed.

Reflection

Truth will out, we are told, and so it repeatedly proves. There may be occasions when deceit goes unnoticed, but falsehood has an uncanny habit of being exposed; of weaving a web that finally traps the very one who spins it. We may suppress the truth, we may twist and distort it, but it is hard to keep it hidden for ever, as the death and resurrection of Christ make crystal clear. His enemies stopped at nothing to get their man, cynically employing false witnesses to secure the verdict they were looking for. Similarly, when they heard news of the empty tomb, they turned once again to deceit, slipping a backhander to the guards in a desperate bid to hush up events. They did all they could to stifle the truth, but it was no good, for first one person, then another, then another still, and so on in perpetuity, met with the risen Lord and knew the truth for themselves.

There is here both challenge and promise. On the one hand, there is a warning that deception will be uncovered however hard we try to conceal it; that all things will finally come to light. On the other hand there is assurance that right will triumph; that God's purpose will emerge victorious. So we put our trust in Christ, the way, the truth and the life, knowing that his love is sure and his mercy dependable, now and always.

Prayer

Lord Jesus Christ,
    forgive me for not always being as truthful as I should be,
    slipping so easily into white lies,
    hiding behind untruths or half-truths,
    or being economical with the truth.
Remind me that *your* truth can set me free,
    and so teach me to receive it with joy,
    speak it in love
    and live by it in faith,
    trusting in your love that alone will never fail.
Amen.

144
Matthew 28:16-20

Still good news

The eleven disciples went to the mountain in Galilee to which Jesus had directed them. On seeing him, they worshipped him, though a few still doubted. Then Jesus appeared, telling them, 'I have been given complete authority in heaven and on earth, so go and make disciples of all people, baptising them in the name of the Father, Son and Holy Spirit, and instructing them to observe everything I have decreed. And never forget that I am constantly by your side, to the very end of time.'

Reflection

Scroll through your TV guide on your remote control at home and you'll be amazed at the astonishing number of TV channels to choose from. Look more closely, however, and something swiftly hits you: many – perhaps even most – of the programmes they advertise are repeats of those previously shown on other channels. We may perhaps want to watch one of two of them again, but with the majority, once you've seen one once you've seen it enough! The great wonder of Easter, by contrast, is that we can repeat its message again and again, yet it goes on being as true and relevant today as it was yesterday, and as it will continue to be tomorrow and the next day, *ad infinitum*.

How different that is from typical modern-day news headlines. I discovered some of those the other day when I was lifting carpets in the course of redecorating. Beneath them were newspapers dating back three, four, even five years, the events emblazoned on the front pages seeming strangely remote. Not that you have to go back years for that to be true; in our high-tech media age, even yesterday's news is old hat. The good news of the resurrection is different. Why? Because it continues to change lives in the present, each day offering hope and new beginnings to believers across the world. Easter Day may be over, but we cannot consign the message it proclaims to the past. It is still good news, today and every day!

Prayer

Sovereign God,
>help me to live each day in the light of Easter,
>with its joy bubbling up in my heart,
>its laughter shining from my eyes,
>its message shaping my life.

So may others, seeing the difference it has made to me,
>discover the difference it can make for them.

Amen.

145
Luke 24:5b
From defeat to victory

'He is not here; he has risen!'

Reflection

'Oh well, that's it,' he said. 'No point in watching any longer.' And it genuinely looked like it. We'd allowed our young son to stay up late that night to watch Manchester United in the European Cup Final but, with the disappointment increasingly evident in his eyes, we were beginning to wish we hadn't. Just a few seconds left – no, actually into injury time – and the German supporters were already saluting their team, the engraver poised over the trophy that was already decked out in their team's ribbons . . . and then it happened: a goal from nowhere, scenes of wild jubilation, and the game heading for extra time. But what was this? Another attack . . . a corner . . . a goal! From the jaws of defeat, Manchester United had snatched victory!

Unbelievable? Well almost. Yet not half so extraordinary as the event nearly two thousand years earlier, when three women made their way solemnly to their master's tomb. There were tears in *their* eyes too; not just of disappointment but of utter devastation, for the one who had been the centre of their lives and on whom they had pinned all their hopes was dead; cruelly murdered on a cross. There was no hope of *him* coming back; it was over, finished. Until suddenly, the tomb was before them . . . empty . . . a stranger telling them Jesus had risen . . . and then, later, the Lord himself standing before them, greeting them as he'd greeted them so often before. Defeat had been turned to victory; a victory not just for them but for us, and one we share in not simply by proxy but first-hand – for it means new life for all, new beginnings, new hope – the assurance that whatever we might face, nothing can stand between us and the love of God in Christ. Unbelievable, yet true!

Prayer

Living God,
> though I may feel crushed beyond redemption,
> teach me that your love will always overcome.

Help me to live each day in the light of what you have done,
> confident that no situation,
> however dreadful it may seem,
> is finally beyond your power to transform,
> and so may I put my trust in you always,
> for this life and the life to come.

Amen.

146
Luke 24:9-11

Too good to be true?

Returning from the tomb, they related everything to the eleven and those gathered with them – it was Mary Magdalene, Joanna, Mary the mother of James, and other women with them who told it to the apostles – but their words seemed like a foolish fancy, and they did not believe them.

Reflection

Do you know the hymn 'Can it be true?' It's not sung today as often as it used to be, which is a pity, for it asks a question central to Easter that many stumble over. The question is essentially this (though the hymn puts it more poetically): can it be true that Jesus lived and died and rose again? Most people have no problems with the first two of those – that Jesus lived and died. But when it comes to resurrection it's a different matter. Quite simply, for many people it seems too good to be true. It's almost as though the very fact that the idea is so special, by definition disproves it. We're just not used to good news like that. It's the stuff of daydreams, not for hard-headed realists of the twenty-first century.

The funny thing is that it wasn't the stuff for hard-headed realists of the first century either. When the women who'd gone to the tomb burst in on the disciples with the news that Christ had risen, their words, so we are told, seemed like a foolish fantasy, or, as the *New International Version* of the Bible so graphically puts it, 'like nonsense'. These were no credulous romantics waiting to swallow any old story; they were down-to-earth individuals, utterly convinced that it was all over; that Jesus was dead and buried. Yet, each came not just to believe but to know that he was alive and with them again through his Spirit; knowledge that was sufficient not just for them to recommit their lives to him but gladly to die in his service. It may have seemed too good to be true, but they were soon to discover that it wasn't. Have you discovered that too?

Prayer

Sovereign God,
    sometimes it *does* seem too good to be true:
    the cross,
    the empty tomb
    and the promise of new life,
    not just now but for all eternity.
Yet, you remind me today that this is precisely how the apostles felt,
    until they met with the risen Christ
    and knew the truth for themselves.
Rekindle my faith this Easter-time.
Assure me, through experiencing again the presence of the risen Christ in my heart,
    that with you nothing is too good to be true,
    for you are able to do more than anyone could ever imagine.
Amen.

147

Luke 24:13-21a

The road to life

That same day, there were two going to a village called Emmaus, about seven miles from Jerusalem, and they were discussing everything that had happened. As they conversed and talked together, Jesus himself drew near and walked with them, but somehow their eyes did not recognise him. He said to them, 'What was it you were discussing together as you walked?' They halted, looking dejected. Then one of them, called Cleopas, answered, 'Are you the only one visiting Jerusalem not to know the things that have happened there over recent days?' 'What things?' he asked. 'The things about Jesus of Nazareth,' they replied. 'A prophet mighty in word and deed before God and all the people; how our chief priests and leaders handed him over to be sentenced to death and then crucified him. We had hoped that he was the one who was going to redeem Israel.'

Reflection

'I'm on the road to nowhere', sang the group Talking Heads in the 1980s, and that's precisely how the two followers of Jesus on the Emmaus Road must have felt. Just a week earlier it had been another story; then they'd made their way to Jerusalem full of hope and expectation, no doubt convinced like the rest of the disciples that the kingdom of God was upon them, that the man they had followed with such fervent devotion was about to take up his throne and rule among them.

How differently, though, things had turned out: instead of being crowned, Jesus had been crucified. And with his death, everything that they'd believed in, worked towards and longed for seemed destroyed. What could the future hold now, for them or anyone? What meaning could there be in life when God had seemingly abandoned them? No doubt they put such questions to the stranger who joined them on the road, so strangely unaware of the awful events that had recently unfolded. It was only when they broke bread together that the penny dropped and their world lurched on its orbit once again. They were on the road after all, not just to Emmaus but to the kingdom of heaven. They were on a journey of discipleship, called still to follow the way of Christ – a pilgrimage we are invited to share in turn, travelling each day in the light of Easter faith.

Prayer

Risen Lord,
> teach me that the journey of life goes beyond this world,
> however special it may be.

Help me to celebrate everything this life has to offer
> and to rejoice in its many blessings,
> but to recognise also that it is but a foretaste of eternity.

May I learn to live each moment in the knowledge that you are
> with me,
> leading me forward,
> whatever I face,
> in life or in death –
> each moment being another step on the road to the joys you
> hold in store,
> now and for evermore.

Amen.

148
Luke 24:22-27
Better than expected

'Furthermore, we were amazed by what some women of our group told us. They went to the tomb at the crack of dawn and couldn't find his body there; but – they told us on their return – in a vision they saw angels, who declared he was alive. Some of our party hurried to the tomb and found things to be precisely as the women had said; but they could see no sign of Jesus.' Then he answered them, 'How foolish you are, and how slow in your hearts to believe everything that the prophets foretold! Is it not the case that the Messiah had to suffer these things before he could enter into his glory?' And he proceeded – starting with Moses and the prophets – to interpret what was said in the Scriptures about him.

Reflection

How often do plans work out as well as you hoped? There may be the odd occasion when they measure up to expectations, but, in my experience, our grand designs and dreams rarely yield in practice what they promise in theory. More often than not, hopes have a habit of falling horribly flat.

A similar sense of anti-climax, though infinitely more intense, was felt by the two disciples walking back along the Emmaus Road, their mood summed up in the plaintive words preceding the passage above: 'We had hoped that he was the one who was going to redeem Israel.' For a time, they had dared to imagine that the promised day of the Lord had dawned, but their hopes had been dashed – another case, so it seemed, of reality not measuring up to expectations. When we read on, though, it's a different story; for suddenly this stranger began to interpret the Scriptures to them, declaring that the death of Jesus was not some ghastly mistake but part of God's redeeming purpose; that the Messiah was not dead but alive; that what the women had told them about the empty tomb was not some foolish fantasy but the glorious, wonderful truth!

Here, in miniature, is one of the great truths of the gospel: that Jesus does not simply fulfil our hopes but far exceeds them, offering joy and peace, hope and strength beyond anything words can begin to express. Thanks be to God!

Prayer

Loving God,
    thank you for everything you have done
    and for everything you have yet to do –
    the blessings I have yet to experience,
    insights I have yet to discover,
    joys you yet hold in store.
Remind me each day that you are able not simply to meet my needs
    but to give me far more than I can ever ask or imagine,
    and so may I look forward in hope,
    living each day joyfully in the light of your love.
Amen.

149
Luke 24:28-32
Light up the fire

As they approached the village they were heading for, he went on ahead of them, apparently intending to continue on his way. Seeing this, they appealed to him, 'Why don't you stay here with us? It's getting late and the night's drawing in.' So he went in and shared lodging with them. When they were settled around a table ready to eat, he picked up some bread, gave thanks for it, and broke it, offering some to them. Suddenly their eyes were opened, and they realised who he was, upon which he disappeared from their sight. Then they said to each other: 'Did not our hearts burn within us as we chatted together on the road and as he opened to us the meaning of the Scriptures?'

Reflection

It only takes a spark, so they say, to get a fire going, and I discovered the truth of that the other day when I went outside to rake out my barbecue. I'd assumed the charcoal would have long since cooled, but although that was true of the top layers, the embers further down were still glowing, easily hot enough to start a new fire had I wished.

Faith, likewise, can grow cold sometimes, all but extinguished by doubts and difficulties. That was certainly true for Cleopas and his companion as they made their way disconsolately back from Jerusalem after the crucifixion of Jesus. As we've seen, their belief that he was the promised Messiah had been crushed, the flame of hope cruelly snuffed out. Or so they'd thought, but suddenly everything changed, as they discovered that death was not the end, evil had not been permitted the last word, hate was not victorious. Doubt and despair gave way to faith and delight; the spark that had seemed thoroughly doused was fanned back into life such that their hearts burned within them as they broke bread with Jesus.

So it can be for us too. Faith at times may splutter, even grow cold, but God is able to fan the smallest spark and rekindle a flame within our heart.

Prayer

Living God,
   speak again to me of your love and purpose,
     move again within me through your restoring, reviving Spirit,
     and from the dying embers rekindle the fire of faith and
     furnace of love.
Whatever life may bring,
   keep alive within me the knowledge that from the tiniest spark of faith
   you are able to set my heart alight once more with joy, wonder, love and praise.
Come then now, and reignite my discipleship,
   so that it may burn brightly for you,
   this and every day.
Amen.

John 20:11-16

Beginnings from endings

Mary stood beside the tomb, sobbing. As she wept, she peered again into the tomb and saw two angels clothed in white sitting where the body of Jesus had previously been lying, one at the head and the other at the feet. They asked her, 'Woman, why are you crying?' She answered, 'They have taken away my Lord, and I have no idea where they have laid him.' Having said this, she turned round and saw Jesus standing there but she did not realise who it was. Jesus said to her, 'Woman, why do you grieve? Who are you looking for?' Imagining he was the gardener, she replied, 'Sir, if you are the one who has carried him off, tell me where you have put him, and I will take him away.' Jesus said to her, 'Mary!' Spinning round, she exclaimed in Hebrew, 'Rabbouni!' (which means Teacher).

Reflection

At first sight, the story of Mary Magdalene in the garden is rather puzzling. How is it that, having been told Jesus has risen, and then seeing him face to face, she doesn't realise who he is? Yet is that really so strange? She'd watched as he drew his last breath on the cross, she'd seen him carried limp and lifeless into the tomb, she'd witnessed the stone being rolled across, and, understandably, she was convinced that it was all over, his life irrevocably extinguished. Anybody who has faced the apparent finality of the death of a loved one will understand those feelings.

Yet slowly the truth dawned: from that ending had come a new beginning, a beginning not just for Jesus but for her and everyone. Joy, hope, purpose, love, which had all been buried with Jesus in the tomb, came leaping back to life; the future that a moment before had seemed so empty was suddenly brimming over with promise. That is the truth of resurrection not just for Mary but also for us all. It does not only speak of life beyond the grave; it tells us that from what looks the bleakest of endings God is able to bring new beginnings beyond our wildest dreams.

Prayer

Lord Jesus Christ,
    teach me, however hopeless circumstances might seem,
    however much I may feel myself to be at a dead end,
    never to lose my sense of all that you are able to do.
Remind me that endings can lead to new beginnings,
    that new life can spring from the old,
    and in that confidence may I look forward to everything you
    will yet do within me.
Amen.

151
John 20:17, 18
A taste of Eden

Jesus told her, 'Do not cling to me, for I have yet to ascend to the Father. Instead, go to my brothers and tell them, "I am ascending to my Father and your Father, my God and your God."' Mary Magdalene went and declared to the disciples, 'I have seen the Lord', after which she shared everything that he had said to her.

Reflection

'In a garden green and gay, all my troubles fade away. Sweet contentment here I find; joy of heart and peace of mind.' Most of us, I'm sure, can relate to those simple words of Patience Strong, but if one person ever had cause to express those sentiments, it was surely Mary Magdalene. She stood sobbing in the garden, her world seemingly at an end, her grief so great that, even when confronted by the empty tomb and the risen Christ, she did not at first realise what was going on. Only slowly, as Jesus called her by name, did the truth dawn: he was alive! His enemies had done their worst . . . and failed. Hatred and evil had seemed victorious, but love had had the final word. For Mary there was indeed joy of heart and peace of mind.

Her story speaks of another garden – Eden – and of God's undoing what took place there. The tree of the knowledge of good and evil has been replaced by the tree of life. Through his dying and rising Jesus has opened the way to Eden for us all. Look back with thanksgiving to Mary's experience in the garden, and look forward with joy of heart and peace of mind to the garden God holds in store.

Prayer

Gracious God,
    I see in the garden of Eden not just Adam and Eve's story
    but mine too,
    for it is my sin,
    my disobedience
    that estranges me from you.
Yet in Mary's garden experience I also see my story,
    for in dying and rising in Christ you have overcome what kept us apart,
    bringing me forgiveness,
    a fresh start,
    new life.
Thank you for the immensity of his sacrifice and wonder of his gift;
    for opening up the gateway to Eden for all.
Amen.

152
John 20:19, 20
A world-changing event

As the day gave way to evening on that first day of the week, and with the disciples having securely fastened doors to the house for fear of the Jews, Jesus appeared and stood among them, saying, 'Be at peace.' Then he showed them his hands and side. On seeing the Lord, the disciples were filled with joy.

Reflection

Which events across the centuries might be said to have changed history? There are many we could choose from: the signing of the Magna Carta, perhaps; Napoleon's defeat at the Battle of Waterloo; the outbreak of the First and Second World Wars; Einstein's publication of the theory of relativity; the discovery of penicillin; the assassination of President Kennedy; the first landing on the moon; the unravelling of DNA, and so we could continue. Claims could be made in relation to numerous occasions across the years, with good justification. Many of them, unquestionably, have powerfully shaped people's lives, for better or worse, but none will have had the far-reaching influence of the resurrection of Christ or the same capacity to change lives for ever. Why? Because we celebrate not simply the one who rose but the one who lives, not just *his* victory over death but *ours* too, not a one-off event but an enduring reality.

That's what Easter is about: life for you, for me, for all; life lived now in a new dimension, transformed by his touch; life that will go on being lived with him for all eternity. It's a message that has shaped countless lives across the world and throughout the ages, and it goes on shaping ours today!

Prayer

Living God,
   joyfully I praise you,
   for you have destroyed the power of death
   and opened the way to life.
Humbly I acclaim you,
   for you have vanquished evil,
   nothing proving able to deny your love.
Gratefully I acknowledge you,
   for you have turned defeat into victory,
   ends into new beginnings.
Reverently I honour you,
   for you have changed life for ever,
   making this and every day a celebration of Easter.
For the triumph you secured,
   and the victory you go on achieving,
   I magnify your holy name,
   through the risen and living Christ.
Amen.

153
John 20:27-29

Beyond doubt

He said to Thomas, 'Put your finger here and see my hands. Reach out your hand and put it in my side. Do not doubt but believe.' Thomas answered him, 'My Lord and my God!' Jesus said to him, 'Have you believed because you have seen me? Blessed are those who have not seen and yet have come to believe.'

Reflection

Few Easter stories are more familiar than that of Thomas, and few seem to speak so emphatically of contrasts, in this case between faith and doubt. Yet are things as straightforward here as they seem? Would the other apostles have reacted any differently in Thomas' place? When Jesus first appeared before them, did they initially believe what their eyes were telling them? An unbiased look at the Easter narratives suggests they did not. The fact is that all struggle to take in the wonder of the resurrection because it runs contrary to everything the world tells us. We want to accept it, yes, but it seems too good to be true.

Are we simply clutching at straws, naively indulging in wishful thinking? Many will accuse us of just that – of swallowing an empty delusion – but despite hostility, ridicule, persecution and controversy, generations across the centuries have continued to trust, personal experience conquering inner doubts. That's what happened for Thomas. His meeting with the risen Christ dispelled his questions and inspired him to kneel instead in grateful worship. For us, too, such a meeting helps us to move from 'Lord, I believe; help me with my unbelief' to sharing in Thomas' joyful acclamation 'My Lord and my God!'

Prayer

Loving God,
    meet with me afresh through the risen Christ,
    and help me to encounter him each day,
    deep within,
    as King of kings and Lord of lords,
    so that my questions may be answered,
    my faith strengthened
    and my doubts overcome.
Nurture my belief,
    and deal with my unbelief.
Amen.

154
John 21:15-17

A second chance

When they had breakfasted, Jesus said to Simon Peter, 'Simon, son of John, do you love me more than these?' He said to him, 'Yes, Lord, you know that I love you.' Jesus said to him, 'Feed my lambs.' He said to him a second time, 'Simon, son of John, do you love me?' He answered, 'Yes, Lord, you know that I love you.' Jesus said to him, 'Look after my sheep.' He asked him a third time, 'Simon, son of John, do you love me?' It wounded Peter that he asked him a third time, 'Do you love me?', so he responded, 'Lord, you know everything; you know that I love you.' Jesus said to him, 'Feed my sheep.'

Reflection

Which of us haven't at some time wished we could have a time over again; that we could undo some thoughtless or angry word, some rash commitment or unwise judgement, or some careless mistake? If only we could have a second chance, an opportunity to put right the past!

If anyone longed for that it must surely have been Peter; for he must have felt helplessly and hopelessly burdened by past mistakes. The memory of his denial of Jesus – not once, not twice, but three times – must have haunted him without respite. What wouldn't he have given to undo those moments? Only, of course, he couldn't – or could he? For suddenly, here was Jesus asking, not once, not twice, but three times: 'Do you love me?' It took a while for the message to sink in, his initial reaction one of pique, but finally, I suspect, the truth dawned – for each time he'd denied him, Jesus was offering the opportunity to make amends, to put the past behind him and start afresh. No, we cannot put the clock back as such, and, yes, sometimes, in terms of others at least, we have to live with the consequences of our mistakes, but with God the opportunity is always there to move forward from what has been towards what shall be. We need only to acknowledge our faults and be truly sorry for resurrection to begin once again, here and now.

Prayer

Gracious God,
    though I try to put the past behind me,
    all too often I am haunted by mistakes.
Though I try to make amends for the wrongs I've done,
    I find it hard to escape a sense of guilt.
Remind me that you are always ready to offer free and total forgiveness,
    no matter how foolish I have been
    or how many opportunities I have wasted.
Teach me that the past is done with
    and the future is open before me.
Receive, then, my thanks
    and lead me forward,
    in the name of Christ.
Amen.

155
1 Corinthians 15:35
The assurance of things hoped for

Some will say, 'How can the dead be raised and what sort of body will they have?'

Reflection

Faith, we are told, is one of the great qualities of the Christian life, an essential ingredient of genuine discipleship. But living with faith is far from easy, for most of us prefer cast-iron certainties to promises we must accept on trust. Nowhere is this more so than when it comes to the fact of death and our hope of eternal life. We believe in the resurrection and the kingdom of heaven, but we can't help wishing we knew a bit more about it. Where will it be? How will we get there? When will it come? What will it be like? These and a host of other questions all too easily play on our minds, insidiously undermining our confidence. 'If only we knew,' we tell ourselves. 'If only we could see, then it would all be so much easier.' But the fact is we do not need to see anything more than God has already revealed, for true faith should be based on what we experience today as much as what we're promised tomorrow. When God is an ever-present reality in our life, we need no proof as to the future.

Prayer

Mighty God,
    teach me to leave all things in your hands,
      trusting for tomorrow through what I know of you today.
Teach me to work for your kingdom
    until that day I enter into the wonder of your presence.
Even when I cannot see you,
    when life seems dark and hope seems to be in vain,
    teach me to keep faith with you
      knowing that you will keep faith with me.
Amen.

156
1 Corinthians 15:51-53
Resurrection promise

Listen and I will tell you a mystery! Not all of us will die, but we will all be changed, in a flash, in the blink of an eye, at the last trumpet. For the trumpet will sound, and the dead will be raised imperishable, and we will be changed. For this ephemeral body must put on an eternal body, and this mortal body must put on immortality.

Reflection

To stand in the presence of death is a sobering experience, especially when the deceased person is a loved one. The features are familiar but the life has gone, the spark that animated them extinguished, and there's nothing we can do to rekindle it. We yearn to see the old familiar smile, a twinkle in the eye and colour in the cheeks, but they are gone, never to return. Few experiences are more painful, and of course grief continues long after the moment of passing; the trauma of bereavement is long term and hard to bear.

For the Christian, though, there's more to death than meets the eye. It's a beginning as well as an end, a fresh page as well as the close of a chapter. Though our loved one may be lost for a time to us, they are never lost to God. His love continues to embrace them and his purpose extends beyond this mortal span. He is able to bring new life from the grave, fuller than anything that has gone before. Alongside grief, there is rejoicing; alongside loss, comfort; alongside despair, hope. That is the message at the heart of the gospel, the promise that gives meaning to our brief span of life. Let us give thanks, then, to God, who gives us the victory, through our Lord Jesus Christ.

Prayer

Loving God,
> hear my prayer for all who mourn.

Reach out to them in their shock, grief, sorrow and loneliness,
> and grant them the comfort you promise,
>> the assurance that death is not the end but the gateway to new life.

May that truth support them as they struggle to come to terms with their loss,
> helping to lessen the sense of emptiness that threatens to overwhelm them.

Speak to them, and me, of the victory of Easter –
> of your love that has defeated the last enemy,
> triumphed over the grave
> and will never let us go.

Amen.

157
1 Corinthians 15:54b-57
Over and done with

'Death has been swallowed up by victory. Where is your victory, death? Where is your sting?' Death's sting is sin, and sin's power lies in the law. Give thanks, then, to God who gives us the victory, through our Lord Jesus Christ.

Reflection

Few words are more instantly recognisable than those of Kenneth Wolstenholme, commentating on the 1966 World Cup Final between England and West Germany. 'They think it's all over', he exclaimed, as fans, believing the match had ended, spilled exuberantly on to the pitch. Then, as Geoff Hurst hammered the ball from distance into the top of the German net to complete a remarkable hat-trick, came the immortal line, '*It is now!*'

Nearly two thousand years earlier a very different scenario was unfolding, in which once again things seemed to be coming towards an end, only this time it was a human life, not a football match. Outside the walls of Jerusalem at a place called Golgotha a man staggered under the weight of a cross, gasped in agony as he was impaled upon it, and groaned in anguish as his life ebbed slowly away. For his followers it must have seemed as though not just his life but also the hopes and faith they had invested in him were at an end too, and any remaining shreds of hope were laid to rest as they watched him cut down and sealed in a tomb. Only, of course, subsequent events were to prove otherwise, for just days later there was to come news of an empty tomb, of Jesus alive, and finally the joy of meeting him face to face, experiencing his presence once more by their sides. They'd thought it was all over, and so it was, but it wasn't life that was finished, it was death!

What had looked like the end was in fact a new beginning. Death had been swallowed up by victory. Thanks be to God, through Jesus Christ our Lord!

Prayer

Living God,
> teach me that you are a God who is constantly able to turn the tables –
> to bring light out of darkness,
> hope out of despair
> and joy out of sorrow –
> a God who has destroyed the hold of sin and death
> and opened the way to life for all,
> life lived now and always with you.

For the assurance that, whatever else may come to an end,
> your love will never finish,
> receive my praise.

Amen.

158

Ephesians 5:14b

Son rise

Awake, you who sleep! Rise up from the dead, and Christ will shine upon you.

Reflection

It was the summer solstice, and once again crowds had gathered to welcome the rising sun. They were a mixed bunch – Druids, New Age devotees and travellers among them – but they were there with a common purpose: to celebrate and give thanks. I don't share their beliefs but I can appreciate their sentiments, for there's no denying that the sun brightens our lives, making everything somehow feel better when it shines. More important, without its life-giving energy this planet of ours would be barren and lifeless, devoid of the wonders we take for granted.

As Christians, though, we celebrate a rising of a different kind: not of the sun but the *Son*. We celebrate the victory of Christ over death; of good over evil, light over darkness and love over hatred. We exult in the empty tomb and the message of the resurrection – good news that changed not just history but the destiny of us all for ever. Here is a rising that shapes everything we are and do; that makes life not only *feel* better but actually *be* better, for it is able to transform lives, including our own. What we are now is never the final word. Our mistakes, our weaknesses, our trials and our sorrows are not the end of the story, for through the risen Christ God offers a new dawn to all. Don't just give thanks today; rejoice *every* day in what he has done for you and for all.

Prayer

Almighty God,
    thank you that in the night-time experiences of life,
    when everything can seem hopeless –
    moments of sorrow, suffering, fear, anxiety, despair and
    disillusionment,
    even death itself –
    you are able to bring a new dawn,
    your light breaking into the darkness
    and shining brightly once more.
May that joyful truth shape everything I think, feel, say and do,
    offering daily encouragement and inspiration,
    until that time when I rejoice for ever in your presence
    and you will be all the light I can ever need,
    for evermore.
Amen.

159
Colossians 1:3-6
Making waves

We always thank God, the Father of our Lord Jesus Christ, because we have heard of your faith, and your love for all the saints, springing from the hope stored up for you in heaven that you heard about in the word of truth, the gospel that has come to you. Just as it has been bearing fruit and growing in the whole world, so, from the moment you first heard it and truly understood the grace of God, it has been bearing fruit among you.

Reflection
When he was a little boy, my son loved throwing stones into water – the bigger the better, since the more exciting the splash they made. Not that it needs a big stone to have a profound effect – just a tiny pebble tossed into the centre of a pool sends ripples radiating inexorably outwards until they reach the bank.

In a sense, the same could be said of the life, death and resurrection of Christ. It all began so quietly, in a stable in Bethlehem and a baby lying in a manger, and, even at the height of his ministry, the majority of the world's population would have been oblivious to his existence. What could one man hope to achieve through his life, death or even resurrection? In global terms, it was a drop in the ocean – but what a drop, for still today the ripples of Christ's coming are reaching outwards! Who would have believed two thousand years ago that the gospel would still be changing lives and the Church continuing to grow? It was beyond his enemies' worst nightmares and greater than his followers' wildest dreams. Yet that is the nature of our God; the God who, in his sovereign power, plunged himself into the pool of human history in such a way that the world would never be the same again.

Prayer

Sovereign God,
 for the power of the gospel –
 the way it has spoken to so many across the centuries;
 for everything you achieved in Christ,
 transforming not just individuals but life itself;
 for your involvement in human history,
 not standing aloof from our need
 but sharing our humanity so that we might share your eternity;
 and for your life-giving grace and mighty strength
 that continue to reach out into the world
 and that will never rest until your will is done and your
 kingdom has come;
 receive my glad and joyful worship.
Amen.

1 Peter 1:3, 4

We've only just begun

Praise be to the God and Father of our Lord Jesus Christ, by whose inestimable mercy we have been born again to a living hope through the resurrection of Jesus Christ from the dead, to an inheritance that is incorruptible, unspoiled and unfading.

Reflection

Back in 1970 The Carpenters had a song in the charts titled 'We've only just begun'. The upbeat title masked a tragic irony, for beneath the surface all was not well with lead singer Karen Carpenter. Just a few years later, in 1974, and aged just 24, she was rushed to hospital, her health undermined by the slimming disease anorexia, and nine years later, following a cardiac arrest, she was dead. Her story cruelly illustrates the promise yet pathos of life. Our brief span on earth offers so much that is special, yet alongside it lurks the spectre of disillusionment, heartbreak, suffering and death, the knowledge that in this life nothing lasts for ever.

And yet the title of that song offers a simple but wonderful synopsis of the message at the heart of the gospel. Whoever we are, whatever we face, God holds out the prospect of a fresh start, of new horizons that beckon us onwards. It's true in *this* life, each day by his grace being a new beginning. It's true even in the face of death, for we have been born again to a new and living hope, of life extending beyond this world to a kingdom that has no end. We live each moment in the context of the God who makes all things new; the God who enables us confidently to declare: we've only just begun.

Prayer

Living God,
    speak to me afresh through the way,
    at the first Easter,
    you brought new beginnings to those whose hopes were dashed
    and whose dreams seemed over.
Remind me of how the risen Christ met them in the upper room,
    in the garden,
    on the road to Emmaus,
    by the waterside,
    on the mountaintop,
    restoring faith and leading them forward to fresh initiatives in your service
    and new experiences of your love.
May I, like them, learn to live each day in the light of your resurrection power,
    assured that, whatever has been, there is more yet to come.
Amen.

ASCENSION DAY

161
Acts 1:6-11
The complete picture

Coming together, they asked him, 'Lord, is this the time when you will restore the kingdom of Israel?' He replied, 'It is not for you to know the time or seasons that the Father has laid down by his own authority, but you will receive power when the Holy Spirit comes upon you and you will be my witnesses both in Jerusalem, and all Judea and Samaria, and to the ends of the earth.' Having said this, and while they were watching, he was lifted up, and a cloud hid him from their sight. While he was going and they were staring into the sky, suddenly two men clothed in white stood next to them. They said, 'Men of Galilee, why do you stand staring into the sky? This Jesus, who has been taken from you up into heaven, will come in the same way that you saw him go.'

Reflection

There are few things worse than reading a book and finding that a page is missing. It's worst of all when it's the last page. Few of us would even start to read a book if we knew it would be cut short, yet, with Jesus, we sometimes do something very similar, celebrating his resurrection, and the gift of his Spirit at Pentecost, but virtually overlooking his Ascension. One reason for this, perhaps, is that our account of the Ascension is caught in a time-warp, reflecting the cosmology of days gone by. God is seen as 'up there' and so Jesus is portrayed as vanishing *up* into heaven, the disciples staring stupefied into the sky. Such language serves to obscure the underlying message of Ascension as surely as the cloud hid Jesus from the apostles' sight.

Yet, if the details of what happened are a mystery, the significance is clear enough. This was a watershed moment for the apostles when they realised, for the first time, the full magnitude of who Jesus was. They had followed him during his ministry, believing him to be the Messiah; they had rejoiced at his resurrection, greeting him as the risen Lord; but now they recognised that he was the Son of God, the King of kings and Lord of all. Don't forget Ascension Day! Above all, don't forget what Ascension Day means, for it reminds us that Jesus is greater than words can begin to express, sovereign over all. It gives us the complete picture, without which our faith is infinitely the poorer.

Prayer

Lord Jesus Christ,
    thank you for the truth at the heart of this day:
    that you were brought low
    yet have been lifted high;
    that you were the servant of all
    yet are above all and beyond all;
    that though you spent your life in Palestine and died in Jerusalem,
    your love has transformed lives in every country and continent,
    crossing barriers of culture, colour and creed.
With all your people in every age,
    I give you praise and glory, honour and thanksgiving,
    now and always.
Amen.

162
Philippians 2:9-11
Glimpsing Christ's glory

God has highly exalted him, giving him the name that is above every name, so that at the name of Jesus every being in heaven, on earth and under the earth should kneel, and every tongue should acknowledge that Jesus Christ is Lord, to the glory of God the Father.

Reflection

The travel writer Bill Bryson gives a memorable account in his book, *The Lost Continent*, of his visit to the Grand Canyon. He arrived there to find the whole area shrouded in freezing fog, so dense that he could barely make out his hand in front of him, let alone the celebrated panorama he'd come to see. Hugely disappointed, he was on the verge of leaving, having waited for as long as his schedule permitted, when suddenly, just for a moment, the fog cleared and there before him stretched a view that left him lost for words. 'Nothing prepares you for the Grand Canyon,' he writes. 'No matter how many times you read about it or see it pictured, it still takes your breath away.'

That experience, for me, takes us to the heart of what the Ascension is all about. Those who had followed Jesus during the course of his ministry, thinking they knew and understood who he was, came to realise at that moment that, in reality, they'd barely understood anything. Even after his resurrection had broken through the fog of doubt and despair, they still saw but a fraction of the full vista rather than the whole. For them, his significance lay in terms of then and there, their own place and time, their own lives and needs. Yet, in the event of the Ascension they came to realise that he was far more than that: the King of kings and Lord of lords, not just for then but for always, not just for them but for everyone, his love, purpose and significance extending for all time and beyond. It was as though the fog suddenly lifted, as though for the first time they saw clearly, recognising that Jesus was greater than they'd ever begun to imagine. Have we grasped that in turn?

Prayer

Lord Jesus Christ,
    thank you for taking on flesh,
    for walking this earth and experiencing first-hand what it means to be human.
Thank you for revealing God in a way I can relate to and understand.
But thank you also that you are more than the man who walked and talked in Galilee;
    that you are one with the Father,
    your love and purpose extending to all.
Help me more fully to grasp that wonder;
    to remember that you are with me
    but also exalted on high,
    a daily friend
    yet the King of kings and Lord of lords.
Amen.

PENTECOST

163
Zechariah 4:6

No contest!

This is the word of the Lord to Zerubbabel: Not by force, nor by authority, but through my Spirit, says the Lord of hosts.

Reflection

In the right corner: Hercules; in the left corner: Mr Bean! It's an incongruous thought, isn't it, a greater mismatch hard to imagine, yet it is no greater than the situation that faced Israel in the days of Zechariah. After many years exiled in Babylon, they had returned to rebuild Jerusalem and restore the temple, but what hope did they realistically have? Compared to the numerous other countries that surrounded them, let alone the mighty empires of their day, they were puny, with scarcely a hope of defending themselves should they be attacked. So it had been for the bulk of their history; a small country surrounded by marauding giants. Humanly speaking, they had no chance, but the words of Zechariah were not about human things but about God and what he could do through his Spirit.

The situation was not so different for the apostles gathered together on the day of Pentecost. How could they possibly fulfil the call of Jesus to make disciples of all nations? The answer, of course, is that *they* couldn't, but *God* could! Without him, they were powerless; with him, all things were possible. We need to remember that truth today whenever we feel up against it. When we look at the needs of society and feel overwhelmed by our inability to respond, when we are faced by apathy concerning the gospel and wonder how we can even begin to share our faith, we need to recall and trust in that promise: 'Not by force, nor by authority, but through my Spirit, says the Lord of hosts.'

Prayer

Sovereign God,
> teach me never to measure a solution by the way things seem
> and never to back away from a challenge because I consider
> myself unable to meet it.

Help me to look to you
> and to trust in your strength that is stronger than any
> earthly power,
> recognising that whatever you set out to accomplish,
> you will do.

Through Jesus Christ my Lord.
Amen.

164
Matthew 28:18, 19
Standby Christians

Jesus drew near and said to them, 'All power in heaven and earth has been given to me. Go, then, and make disciples of all people, baptising them in the name of the Father, the Son and the Holy Spirit.'

Reflection

Did you know that the power used to keep televisions and electrical appliances in the UK on standby for just one day would be sufficient to provide electricity for a small town? It's a sobering thought, isn't it, all that power going to waste, achieving nothing.

Perhaps equally sobering is the thought that we as individuals and, together, as a Church, might be guilty of wasting a different sort of power – the power of God. 'You will receive power,' said Jesus, 'when the Holy Spirit comes upon you.' What he envisaged there was the power of the Spirit so flowing through us that we shall make a difference to the world we live in, changing lives through our work and witness. Some, of course, do just that, but, all too often, our efforts are devoted simply to keeping our own affairs ticking over. We look to our own journey of discipleship, our own relationship with Christ, and no further. As churches, we look inwards rather than outwards, concerned with servicing our plethora of committees, maintaining the fabric and supporting church events. Instead of surging out, God's power becomes trapped in an internal loop. It is as though we, too, are put on standby, rarely if ever used for the purpose we were designed for.

If the power stored in all those appliances on standby could meet the needs of a town, so the power at our disposal could meet the needs of the world, if only we had the will and courage to release it.

Prayer

Living God,
> forgive me for being so concerned with myself
> that I forget my responsibility to others.

Forgive the narrowness of my vision that has led me to become a
> holding station rather than conduit of your renewing grace.

Move within me,
> and open my life to all that you are able to do,
> so that your power may flow in me,
> through me
> and from me,
> to the glory of your name.

Amen.

165
Acts 2:1-4, 16-18a
A gift for all

When the day of Pentecost dawned, they were gathered in one place. Suddenly, a sound like the rush of a mighty wind came from heaven, filling the house where they were sitting. After that, tongues of fire appeared that divided, so that a tongue rested on each of them. They were all filled with the Holy Spirit, and began to speak in various tongues, as the Spirit enabled them. This is what was spoken of by the prophet Joel: 'In the last days, God declares, I will pour out my spirit on all people; your sons and daughters will prophesy, your old men will dream dreams, and your young men will see visions. I will pour out my spirit even on male and female slaves in those days.'

Reflection

Have you stayed in the Hilton hotel, owned a Rolls-Royce or dined with the Queen? I haven't, and I very much doubt I ever will. Some things in life are reserved for the select few, while the majority of us have to make do with more run-of-the-mill facilities and occasions.

The people of the Old Testament believed that this was true of the Spirit of God, being convinced that it was a rare and special gift which only a privileged elite would experience. There was no way in the world *they* would be filled by that Spirit; such an honour went to those like Gideon, Samuel, Isaiah, Ezekiel and others of similar stature. For the rank and file, God would always be one step removed, access to him mediated by priest and temple. The words of the prophet Joel, wonderful though they sounded, must have raised more than a few eyebrows when first spoken, for they postulated an entirely new relationship with God.

Yet that is the relationship experienced by the apostles on the so-called day of Pentecost, and it is a gift offered to us in turn. God is not remote and detached, but can be experienced as a living reality within – encouraging, teaching, empowering, guiding – ever at work in our lives. There is no favouritism with God. There is one privilege we can all enjoy: the inner presence of the Holy Spirit – surely the greatest privilege of all!

Prayer

Holy Spirit,
    unpredictable as the wind
    unquenchable as fire,
    yet gentle as a dove,
    come now and breathe new energy into my life
    and new life into my soul,
    by your gracious power.
Amen.

166
2 Corinthians 3:17
Gloriously free

Now the Lord is the Spirit, and there is freedom wherever that Spirit of the Lord is.

Reflection

I watched them in fascination – wind-surfers riding the waves back and forth across the water, now tacking against the breeze, now going with it, spray tossed up all around them as they raced at astonishing speed across the swell. I've never had the courage to give it a go – I doubt I ever will – but it must be an exhilarating experience, ducking, diving, twisting and turning in harmony with the elements. Not only must that uplift the body, it must also stir the spirit, bringing a sense of excitement and, above all, unprecedented freedom. No longer is the power of the wind and waves something to be fought against; rather, it is harnessed, identified with, celebrated.

The Apostle Paul talks of a different kind of freedom, but in similarly glowing terms. He has in mind the liberty we experience as Christians through God's Spirit, one that has many facets. It means freedom from guilt and shame, from the need to make amends for our actions and in some way earn pardon, for we are assured of God's grace and mercy. It means freedom from fear, whether of worldly troubles or of death itself, for we know he is with us in whatever we face, nothing able to separate us from his love. It means freedom from whatever holds us captive; freedom to be ourselves and to live life to the full; for that is what God has promised: abundant and overflowing life for all eternity. The waves of life will still toss us about, but through opening our hearts to the wind of God's Spirit we can ride with and above them, celebrating the glorious liberty he makes possible for all.

Prayer

Loving God, thank you for the freedom I experience through
  your Spirit.
You have delivered me from whatever denies and diminishes life,
  filling me instead with love,
  life,
  laughter,
  light.
Teach me to celebrate each day the glorious freedom of loving
  and knowing you,
  and joyfully to surf the waves of your grace
  on the wind of your Spirit.
Amen.

167
Romans 8:26, 27
Partners in prayer

In the same way, the Spirit identifies with us in our weakness. We do not know how to pray or what to pray for, but the Spirit pleads on our behalf with entreaties that are beyond words, and the one who searches our hearts knows the Spirit's mind, because he intercedes constantly on behalf of the saints seeking the fulfilment of God's purpose.

Reflection

A while back, I was asked to speak at an event for Christian leaders on the subject of personal prayer. The invitation came as something of a surprise, for although I have written innumerable prayers, I still consider myself anything but an expert on the subject. Like the vast majority of Christians, prayer does not always come easily to me, nor am I as disciplined about it as I should be. If my spiritual well-being and relationship with God were entirely down to me, frankly it wouldn't be up to much. Thankfully, it's not; neither for me nor any one of us.

The Holy Spirit articulates our thoughts to God, even when *we* find it impossible to do so. More than that, Christ himself is constantly interceding on our behalf, bringing our unspoken needs and requests before God. Prayer may start with us but it doesn't end there. However much it may sometimes feel like it, we are never alone when we attempt to pray. That's not to encourage casualness or complacency, for prayer is ultimately given for our own benefit as much as God's, but if you can't quite find the right words, and if you genuinely can't find the time you'd like to give, don't punish yourself, your prayer will get to him nonetheless.

Prayer

Living God,
 there are times when I pray but the words just won't come,
 and times when I simply don't know what to pray for.
Thank you that I am not alone in prayer;
 that your Spirit works within,
 articulating my deepest thoughts and needs,
 and constantly interceding on my behalf through Christ.
When I cannot say the things I mean or want to,
 speak for me,
 through your Spirit.
Amen.

168

1 John 3:24b

With him in Spirit

We know that he lives in us by the Spirit that he has put within us.

Reflection

If only we could share the experience of the disciples, following Jesus through the streets of Galilee and the hills of Palestine during the course of his earthly ministry, and meeting him again as the risen Lord in the days after his resurrection. Have you ever thought that? Do you ever feel sometimes that, compared to them, we're at a disadvantage, denied the privilege of seeing him face to face, hearing his words and witnessing his deeds? That's absolutely true, so far as it goes . . . only it doesn't go far enough. True, Jesus is not physically here beside us, but he is with us nonetheless in a way more special still: present through his Holy Spirit deep within.

Tragically, that gift of the Spirit has been the subject of untold controversy within the Church, too often causing suspicion, hostility, bitterness and division – the very opposite of what God intended. Why has this happened? Because undue emphasis has been placed on the gifts rather than *gift* of the Spirit. The result has been to portray the Holy Spirit as the preserve of a few Christians rather than the experience of all, yet that's not what Jesus taught. 'I will ask the Father,' he told his disciples, 'and he will give you another comforter to be with you for ever' (John 14:16). The promise is for us all: when we acknowledge Christ as Lord and commit ourselves to his way, his Spirit is with us, making his presence real within. True, we don't get to walk and talk with Jesus quite as his followers did during his earthly ministry, but we can know him nonetheless, not only by our side but also in our heart. Could we really want more?

Prayer

Spirit of God,
    mysterious and indefinable,
    moving in ways beyond my predicting or control,
    thank you for the guidance, instruction and insight you daily give;
    for the ways you challenge and inspire,
    nurturing and nourishing my faith
    and equipping me for service;
    for making Christ real within me
    so that I can know him for myself
    and experience the reality of God's love within my heart.
Move within me afresh
    and open my life to the ways you seek to work.
Fill, renew, shape and transform me,
    this and every day.
Amen.

TRINITY SUNDAY

169
John 16:12-15
The complete picture

'There is still much that I have to tell you, but you're not yet ready for it. The Spirit of truth will lead you into truth when he comes, speaking not on his own behalf but communicating what he hears and declaring to you what is to come. Through sharing my words with you he will bring me glory. Everything that belongs to the Father belongs also to me. So it is that I have told you he will take what is mine and make it known to you.'

Reflection

The putt seemed relatively short and the green looked to be completely flat, but the television picture was misleading. Not only was the shot all of eight feet but it was down a surprisingly sharp slope, which caused the ball to race alarmingly past the hole. That's the trouble with seeing things in only two dimensions – it gives a partial picture that can be highly deceptive. It's not for nothing that television and film producers have spent years developing 3D cameras and the like, though whether the rigmarole of putting on the special glasses required to enjoy the 3D experience will ever catch on I'm not convinced.

Trinity Sunday reminds us that three dimensions are equally important when it comes to God. We speak rightly of God being almighty, omnipotent, the creator of the ends of the earth, but if we see him as only this then our picture is incomplete. We speak rightly of God in human form, walking our earth, sharing our joys and sorrows, experiencing temptation just as we do, but, once more, if we imagine this gives us the complete picture we're sadly mistaken. We speak rightly of God being Spirit, his power at work in the world, his presence experienced within, but though this is also a perfectly valid picture of God, to take it in isolation would be to settle for a one-dimensional view that ultimately muddies the waters. We struggle to get our heads round the strange-sounding idea of God being three in one yet one in three, yet however nonsensical it sounds, we cannot do without it, for only when we see God as at once Father, Son and Holy Spirit do we begin to glimpse the complete picture.

Prayer

God the Father,
>   mighty and mysterious,
>   greater than I can ever comprehend –
>   for sustaining the universe,
>   creating life
>   and shaping the course of history,
>   I praise you.

God the Son,
>   for taking on flesh,
>   experiencing what it means to be human
>   even to the point of suffering and death,
>   I thank you.

God the Holy Spirit,
>   for working in human lives,
>   teaching, equipping, renewing and empowering,
>   I acclaim you.

Awesome and wonderful God,
>   three in one yet one in three,
>   help me always to see you in all your glory
>   rather than in the single dimension I all too easily reduce you to.

Amen.

170
1 Corinthians 12:4-6
A glorious mystery

Now there are various gifts, but the same Spirit; various ministries but the same Lord; different types of service but the same God working through all of them.

Reflection

Mention Advent, Christmas, Holy Week or Easter to most Christians, and you will see a sparkle of interest in their eyes, for these are well-loved festivals that speak in innumerable ways. Mention Trinity Sunday and you are more likely to witness a blank expression or complete lack of interest. It is an occasion that few people warm to, and one that in many nonconformist churches passes completely unnoticed. Why?

You only need to look at the so-called Athanasian Creed to find out the answer. It goes like this: 'I believe in God the Father incomprehensible, God the Son incomprehensible, God the Holy Spirit incomprehensible' and so on, at great length. For many people the word 'incomprehensible' sums up both this creed and the ideas about God it is trying to express. When it comes to the doctrine of the Trinity, we are out of our depth, struggling with concepts that baffle us, for how can it make sense to talk of three persons who are at once wholly distinct yet wholly one? It is, indeed, incomprehensible.

Yet that is the whole point, the very reason why Trinity Sunday is so important, for it reminds us of a truth we cannot afford to forget: that God is beyond the human intellect, defying expression, greater than we can ever conceive. We encounter him as a loving Father who is yet sovereign over all; as a human being who lived and died among us yet rose again and is exalted at the Father's right hand; and as an inner reality that fills us with peace, joy, hope and power.

We cannot explain how the pieces fit together but we know that they do, for we have experienced the truth for ourselves. If we imagine that we have solved the mystery and that the full wonder of God is firmly in our sights, then it is time to think again, for if we ever think that, then the truth is that we have lost sight of him altogether.

Prayer

Mighty God,
    beyond all space and time,
    greater than my mind can grasp,
    ruler over all that is, has been and shall be –
    I worship you.
Loving Father,
    kind and merciful,
    full of goodness and compassion,
    constantly watching over me and directing my steps –
    I praise you.
Saviour Christ,
    flesh of my flesh yet the living image of God,
    sharing my humanity yet one with the Father,
    loving to the point of death yet bringer of life –
    I acknowledge you.
Holy Spirit,
    free and mysterious,
    source of guidance and inspiration,
    filling my heart and mind –
    I welcome you.
Mighty God,
    Father, Son and Holy Spirit,
    with awe, joy and thanksgiving I celebrate all you mean to me
    and everything you have done in my life.
Amen.

HARVEST

171
Genesis 1:26
Caring for God's world

Then God said, 'Let us create humankind in our likeness, our image; and let them have authority over the fish of the sea, birds of the air, cattle and every wild creature, including everything that creeps upon the earth.'

Reflection

The land was an oasis of tranquillity in the heart of a vast urban sprawl, a sparkling jewel set in the heart of a concrete jungle that stretched for miles along the coastline. Cows grazed the meadows, footpaths meandered across the cliff-top, hedgerows resounded to a chorus of bird song and wild flowers bloomed in a sea of colour. Had the area not been bequeathed years earlier to the National Trust, it too would probably have succumbed to the developers and been covered over by yet more luxury apartments, but happily, thanks to the generosity and vision of generations past, it had been saved for posterity.

For too long the Church was silent on issues concerned with the environment; indeed, the nonconformist work ethic made certain denominations complicit in the thoughtless plundering of this earth's resources. Recent years, though, have seen a change, as theologians increasingly draw our attention to the ecological implications of faith. As Psalm 24:1 reminds us, 'The earth is the Lord's and everything in it.' This planet is given not just to *us* but to *all*; a gift to nurture rather than possession to exploit. We have a responsibility to God and to others, the world in all its beauty and variety being held by us in trust. Forget that and we'll not just deprive future generations but we'll all ultimately be the loser.

Prayer

Creator God,
> you have placed in humankind's hands the welfare of this planet,
> a gift beyond price.

Yet too often we have abused your creation,
> despoiling, plundering, wasting and abusing.

Instead of seeing it as a gift we have viewed it as ours by right;
> instead of acting as faithful stewards we have acted carelessly
> and thoughtlessly,
>
> repeatedly frittering away the riches you have entrusted to us.

Forgive my share in squandering its resources,
> living today with no thought of tomorrow or of present and
> future generations.

Teach me to live more responsibly,
> and inspire others to do the same.

Amen.

172
Psalm 24:1; 95:4

The call to conserve

The earth is the Lord's and everything in it, the world and all those who live in it. In his hand are the innermost parts of the earth, and the mountain peaks belong to him. The sea is his, for he made it, and his hands shaped the dry land.

Reflection

I was reading an article in *The Ecologist* the other day that somehow gave me a new perspective on the story of Noah's flood. It was nothing revolutionary: simply the observation that God commanded Noah to take two of every living creature into the ark. What was the reason for that? The truth, surely, is that not only humankind but the whole of creation matters to God. It is not ours to exploit willy-nilly, as we sometimes seem to imagine; he has a place in his heart for everything he has made. Do we as Christians take that seriously? We may think we do, but how many of us show it in the way we live.

There seems little doubt that the world today is in the grip of a growing ecological crisis. Sadly, the response from the Church has typically been muted, one Christian even suggesting to me that such matters should not concern us since our future is in heaven rather than on earth. I, for one, cannot accept such a simplistic response. Indeed, I wonder sometimes if those who call us to wake up to our environmental responsibilities, whether they be Christian or otherwise, are the true prophets of our time. If the earth is the Lord's, as we claim, then do we not owe it to him to take care of it, if not for our sakes then for his?

Prayer

Sovereign God,
> forgive me for so often abusing all you have given –
> despoiling this world,
> failing to appreciate it as I should,
> treating it as mine by right rather than entrusted as your gift.

Teach me to see it not as a trinket or a plaything
> but as a priceless treasure –
> an heirloom passed on to me
> and to be handed on intact to others.

So, teach me to live wisely and responsibly,
> in harmony with you and all you have made.

Amen.

173
Psalm 95:3-7a
Stewards of creation

The Lord is a great God, a great king over all gods. In his hands are the depths of the earth, as well as the hills and valleys. The sea is his, he made it, together with the dry land, fashioned by his hands. Come! Let us prostrate ourselves in worship, let us kneel before the Lord who made us, for he is our God and we are his people, the flock that he shepherds.

Reflection

Probably few people were overly surprised when George W. Bush, on his accession to the US presidency, promptly cancelled American support for the Kyoto agreement on greenhouse gases and climate change. Given his record as a state governor, it was pretty much par for the course, yet even the most hardened observers must have caught their breath at the stunning cynicism of his actions. The world today is facing intolerable pressures, and the threat of ecological catastrophe is all too real, yet the richest country in the world, responsible for well over half of all greenhouse gas emissions, saw fit to turn its back on the most important international agreement on the environment so far negotiated.

The reason? Money. And there, in a nutshell, is the issue at the heart of environmental change. Most of us claim to be concerned about the environment, yet we baulk when it comes to paying more for a truly green product. We say we abhor waste, yet make little effort to recycle rather than throw things away. We wring our hands over pollution, yet we think nothing of hopping into the car rather than walk or cycle. If we really believe this is God's world held by us in trust, can we ever justify such carelessness? As Christians, we not only need to add our voices to the mounting calls for a sensible stewarding of creation; we also need to live in such a way that we give a lead through our actions. To fail in that is to betray the responsibility God has placed into our hands.

Prayer

Lord of all,
> forgive me my part in a society that has too often lived
> for today with no thought of tomorrow.

Forgive my acceptance of an economic system that plunders this
> world's resources with little regard as to the consequences.

Help me to live less wastefully
> and with more thought for those who will come after me.

Challenge the hearts and minds of people everywhere,
> that both they and I may understand more fully the wonder
> and fragility of this planet,
> and so may we honour our calling to be faithful stewards of
> it all.

Amen.

174
Hosea 8:7a; 10:12a
Consider what you sow

They sow the wind and reap the whirlwind. Sow righteousness and you will reap steadfast love.

Reflection

Have you ever planted something and then wished you hadn't? It's easily done. One look at a seed catalogue or book on plants and it's hard to resist splashing out in the hope of creating a tapestry of fragrance and colour in your own back garden. The trouble is that many plants are entirely unsuited to small spaces: some grow far too tall, others prove invasive, and others produce so many seeds that they're almost impossible to eradicate once they become established. It pays to consider carefully the things you sow and grow.

The same applies to life in general, for there, too, more often than not, we reap what we sow. Unkind words and thoughtless deeds lead to strained relationships, carelessness to accidents, laziness to missed opportunities, pride to a fall, and so we could continue. So much of what we do, say or think has a habit of rebounding on us, for better or for worse. And, more disturbingly, once we allow a seed to germinate – whether it's a fault here or mistake there – the result can take on a life of its own, like a pernicious weed that's hard to remove once it's taken root. Whatever, then, you allow to grow in your life, consider first the likely harvest.

Prayer

Father God, forgive me,
    for all too often I live carelessly,
        having little thought not only for you but also for others.
I speak without thinking,
    act with little thought as to the consequences,
    and then wonder why my mistakes return to haunt me.
Instead of joy I bring sorrow;
    instead of harmony, discord;
    instead of help, hindrance;
    instead of encouragement, dismay.
Teach me, Lord, that in so many ways I reap what I sow,
    for good or ill.
Help me, in everything I do,
    to be more caring,
    more considerate,
    more supportive,
    more wise,
    so that the harvest of my life may be pleasing to you.
Amen.

175

Mark 4:2-9

An unlikely harvest

Jesus told the crowd many parables, including this one: 'A farmer went out to sow and, as he did so, some seed fell by the wayside, and the birds swooped down and devoured it. Other seed fell on rocky ground, where there was little soil, and though it sprang up quickly, when the sun rose it was baked and withered away, since it had no root. Other seed fell among thorns, which, as they grew, choked the seedlings, so that they yielded no grain. Other seed fell into good soil and brought forth grain, rising up and increasing and yielding thirty and sixty and a hundredfold.' And he said, 'Let those with ears to hear listen!'

Reflection

Reading the parable of the sower, one question – for me at least – inevitably springs to mind: why wasn't the farmer in question more careful about where he sowed his seed? After all, seed doesn't come cheaply, and I'm sure that farmers then, as much as now, would have been eager to maximise their profit margins, so why not plough and till the soil until there was no risk of any seed falling among weeds or on stony ground? It's not that simple, of course, as I've often noticed while out walking. Frequently I've come across fields that seem to be more stones than soil, despite the farmer's best efforts. Yet, somehow, such fields succeed year on year in yielding a full and healthy crop.

Never lose heart, then, when it comes to sowing the seed of God's word. It may seem, looking at today's world, that we are faced with hopelessly stony ground that offers little prospect of the Christian message taking root in people's lives, but the fact is that God time and again overturns expectations, speaking to those we least anticipate, cultivating fruit in the most unlikely of lives.

What to us may seem a barren wilderness to him can be a field ready for planting. The final harvest is out of our hands, but sowing the seed is very much in them, and the results may well surprise us.

Prayer
Father God,
>help me to recognise that the seed of your word can germinate
>in unexpected places,
>challenging those I least expect
>and transforming lives in ways I can scarcely credit.

Wherever it sown,
>nurture and nourish it
>so that it may yield a rich and fruitful harvest.

Amen.

176
Galatians 5:22
Spring blossom

The fruits of the Spirit are love, joy, peace, tolerance, compassion, goodness, faithfulness, gentleness and self-discipline. Nothing can legislate against things like these.

Reflection

A sight I look forward to each year is that of spring blossom. Suddenly trees and shrubs that had looked drab and ordinary are transformed into things of beauty. Not only is the blossom special in its own right, but it also promises fruit that, in time, will be harvested; the delicate flowers are the first steps in a process that will hopefully culminate in a rich harvest.

Whenever I read the words of Paul concerning the fruits of the Spirit, I'm acutely aware that the yield I produce is lacking, few if any such fruits being evident in any quantity. No doubt you, likewise, long to be more gentle, patient, loving, kind, understanding, merciful, calm and the like. Sadly, the soil in our lives tends to be infinitely less fertile than it could or should be. That's part of being human and, as a result, the crop we produce repeatedly falls short. But though we may fail to attain a bumper harvest, with God's help we can at least show signs of spiritual growth, his Spirit working within us to produce, if not fruit, then blossom, promising more yet to come.

Prayer

Gracious God,
    nurture my faith,
    nourish my discipleship,
    and grant that in the fullness of time buds may burst into bloom
    and my life may bear living fruit in your service,
    testifying to your transforming love and redeeming grace.
Though I will always fall short,
    grant that something of your beauty may grow within me.
Amen.

177
Galatians 6:7-9
Reaping what we sow

Do not be taken in: God will not be made a fool of. Whatever someone sows, that person will also reap; the one who sows what the body wants will reap corruption, but the one who sows what the Spirit desires will reap eternal life through that same Spirit. So, then, let us never grow weary of doing what is right, for, provided we do not give up, we will reap at harvest-time.

Reflection

Several years back, my wife took a fancy to the Welsh poppy, deciding that it was something we ought to grow, so every time we visited a garden centre, we looked for a specimen. Eventually, we found one and with eager anticipation we planted it in the border. We were not disappointed; the plant flowered its heart out for month after month. The following year, though, we were in for a shock, for suddenly we didn't have *one* Welsh poppy, we had *hundreds* – another sprouting, so it seemed, wherever we cared to look! Here was a classic case of reaping what you sow, even if we hadn't physically scattered the seeds ourselves. A little more research and we would have known exactly what we were letting ourselves in for.

How far, though, can we apply this principle to life? Hard work is not always rewarded, honesty doesn't always pay, effort doesn't guarantee success, and love doesn't guarantee love in return. Yet, having said that, there is another level at which we *do* reap what we sow, both in this life and beyond. The rewards associated with Christian discipleship may not be tangible, but they are there nonetheless. The rewards for loving others, offering our service and pursuing good may not be quantifiable in human terms, but they are no less real. Similarly, wrongdoing and injustice, though they may seem to go unpunished, carry their own cost. We can sow with no thought of tomorrow if we wish – God will not stop us – but he tells us repeatedly throughout the Scriptures that the time will come, whether in this life or the next, when we will reap the harvest. What, then, will we sow? It's our choice.

Prayer

Sovereign God,
    teach me, despite the apparent contradictions of life,
    to keep faith that you are there,
        striving against everything that frustrates your will
        and denies your love.
Teach me to hold on to those moments when I see wrongs righted
    and justice done.
Above all, teach me to look at the cross of Christ
    and to draw strength from the victory there of love
    over what had seemed to be the triumph of evil.
Amen.

ALL SAINTS' DAY

178
Philippians 3:17
A rare breed

Dear friends, imitate my example and, in turn, learn from those who follow the pattern we have given.

Reflection

They lined the marshes, a great throng of birdwatchers, peering through binoculars and telescopes, or painstakingly adjusting their gigantic zoom lenses in the hope of catching that definitive close-up shot. Each looked out to sea eagerly, expectantly, the air of excitement almost palpable, and yet more people were regularly arriving to swell their ranks. What was it all about? A rare species of gull had been spotted there earlier in the week, presumably blown off course by winter storms. There was nothing particularly special about it, certainly nothing dramatic, yet these twitchers were in seventh heaven, delighted to have the opportunity to tick yet another bird off their list of unusual sightings.

We might not get worked up ourselves by a brief glimpse of an uncommon bird, but the Apostle Paul points us towards rarities of another sort that we *should* get excited about. He was referring, of course, to those special people who set an example to follow; specifically those like himself who provide others with a model of faith, exemplifying Christian commitment. In the early Church there were many to choose from, numerous believers who sacrificed their all for the cause of Christ. Others have joined them across the years, surrendering prospects, possessions, livelihoods, even life itself for the sake of the gospel. Others again have offered an example of a different sort, displaying a depth of wisdom, love and compassion that has brought inspiration to others and encouraged them in their own journey of discipleship. Today is a day for remembering those special people, the recognised and unrecognised saints of God. It is a day for learning from them, and a day also for seeking to emulate their lives so that we likewise, in some small way, may set an example ourselves.

Prayer

Almighty God,
    thank you for those whose lives have shone out as a beacon
    of light,
    the breadth of their insight,
    sincerity of their love,
    quality of their character
    and extent of their goodness being unmistakable to all.
Thank you for those who have inspired me personally,
    helping to fire and strengthen my faith,
    to guide, nurture, teach and encourage.
Help me to learn from their example
    so that I may grow each day a little closer to the fullness
    of Christ
    and perhaps, somehow, inspire others in turn.
Amen.

179
Hebrews 12:1, 2
Running together

So then, since we are surrounded by so great a crowd of witnesses, let us discard everything that encumbers us and the sin that clings so closely, and let us run with perseverance the race set before us, looking to Jesus, the beginning and end of our faith, who, focusing on the joy set before him, endured the cross, disregarding its shame, and has taken his seat at the right hand of the throne of God.

Reflection

A memorable sight each year is that of the massed ranks of runners assembled for the London marathon, a scene echoed on a smaller but similarly impressive scale at numerous other long-distance events across the country. A select band in the field run seriously, striving to beat the other competitors after months of punishing training, but the majority will take part simply for fun, frequently to raise much-needed funds for charity. Far from competing against each other, they run together, the race being a shared experience undertaken in a spirit of unity.

The same holds true in terms of faith. Our race is not one in which we strive to outdo each other. Rather, we participate alongside a great company of saints, past, present and future, from whom we can draw encouragement and inspiration that we pass on to others in turn. Reflect, then, on those who have gone before you, consider those who will come after, and give thanks for those who run with you now, recognising what you can receive from them and also give. You'll struggle to run the race on your own, for it is a marathon, not a sprint. You need to hold on to the knowledge that you are part of something bigger than yourself, part of a great company engaged in the same undertaking, serving the same Lord and seeking the same goal.

Prayer

Gracious God,
> thank you that I do not run the race of Christian discipleship on my own,
> but am part of an ongoing procession that extends far back across the years
> and will continue long after I have finished my course.

Thank you for those who have gone before me,
> especially those who have displayed special faith and dedication.

Thank you for those across the world who follow you today,
> seeking to follow in Christ's footsteps and be true to his way.

Thank you for those with whom I share fellowship,
> together with those whose words, deeds, teaching or ministry
> have helped to give me strength and support in my own journey of faith.

Above all, thank you for your Son, Jesus Christ,
> who so faithfully ran the race you set before him
> and waits at the finishing line to welcome me home.

Teach me to learn from him and from others,
> so that I may run my own race as faithfully as I can
> and in some small way help others to run theirs in turn.

Amen.

180
Hebrews 13:5
All saints

Remember your leaders, those who spoke the word of God to you; consider the outcome of their way of life, and imitate their faith.

Reflection

In 1492, as we will all have learnt at school, Christopher Columbus set off from Spain in the *Santa María*, sailing west on a journey that he hoped would take him around the world to India. His crew were terrified, convinced that, since the earth was flat, they would eventually fall off the edge to their deaths. Of course, nobody fell off anywhere, the ship eventually reaching what came to be known as the West Indies. The destination may have been other than intended, but the voyage proved conclusively that the world was not flat at all but round. Once done, many followed the same journey, and a thriving trade route was soon established. As so often in life, it took someone to show the way, someone to convince the doubters of what could be done.

That, for me, takes us to the heart of All Saints' Day, a day that celebrates those who have gone before us in faith, and whose Christian discipleship has inspired subsequent generations. It's not about holier-than-thou men and women adorned by a halo, such as we might see in a church stained-glass window, but about ordinary people like you and me whose lives serve as an extraordinary example. Remember such people, take note of their way of life, and learn from them, for they have shown what can be done and what God waits to do, here and now, in your life today.

Prayer

Living God,
> encourage me through all who have walked with you before me,
> so that I in turn may encourage those who come afterwards.

Teach me to learn from the great company of saints,
> so that my love for you may grow,
> my faith be deepened
> and my resolve to serve you be strengthened.

So may I live always to your praise and glory,
> through Jesus Christ my Lord.

Amen.

REMEMBRANCE DAY

181
Psalm 44:1, 7a
Lest we forget

We have heard for ourselves, O God, our predecessors have told us the deeds you performed in their time, how in bygone days you saved us from our enemies.

Reflection

'Do you remember the time we came here before?' asked my mother. I racked my brains, trying to recall it, but it was no good; the occasion was clean forgotten, as though it had never been. We do remember many things, of course, but we forget many others, as probably all of us can testify from bitter experience. Points we ought to remember have that infuriating habit of disappearing from our minds just when we need to recall them most, and so we resort to such props as a knot in a hankie or a memo-board in the kitchen, hoping that these may jog our memory.

Such, increasingly, is the rationale behind Remembrance Day. Every year, the number of those who lived through one or both of the two World Wars diminishes, yet for that reason the occasion becomes more rather than less important. We have only to witness the horrors of Bosnia, or the continuing violence in the Middle East and so many other parts of the world, to realise that things haven't changed as much as we might like to think. Some even dare to suggest that the horrors of the Holocaust never actually happened, thus dismissing, at a stroke, the suffering, terror and anguish experienced by so many millions. The fact is that we cannot afford to forget the past. Remembrance Day does not glorify war but rather recalls the price of peace, reminding us of the evil and inhumanity that people can stoop to, and the sacrifice so many made to ensure that such tyranny did not triumph. It purposely thrusts such things back into our consciousness – lest we forget.

Prayer

Almighty God,
> on this day of remembering,
> help me to learn the lessons of the past:
> to understand the cost of war,
> the price of peace,
> the scope of human depravity
> and the extent of human self-sacrifice.

Help me to learn those lessons –
> to live and work for peace,
> to stand up against evil,
> to serve and not to count the cost,
> to work in whatever way I can for a better world.

Forgive me that I do not remember as often as I should,
> forgetting how fortunate I am to live in freedom and how lucky to enjoy peace;
> forgetting those who still suffer from the wounds of battle
> and others who even now mourn their loved ones.

Speak to me today
> and help me not only to say the words but truly to mean them:
> 'We will remember them.'

Amen.

182
John 15:13
A debt owed

'There is no greater love than this: to give your life for another.'

Reflection

During my time with the movement Toc H I was privileged to visit the battlefields of the First World War, visiting in particular the countless war cemeteries around the towns of Ypres and Poperinge. There can surely be few more salutary sights, or more powerful reminders of the awful consequences of war. The number of people buried in that area alone runs into hundreds of thousands and, of course, the names of countless others are recorded on the Menin Gate in tribute to those whose bodies were never found. A small proportion of those who died were in their thirties and forties, but the overwhelming majority were younger: twenty-something or less. In one cemetery there is even a grave of a fourteen-year-old, one of the numerous lads who lied about their age in order to enlist. And all this is not to mention to innumerable others who were injured in the conflict, maimed or scarred for the rest of their lives. Scenes and statistics like these remind us of the dreadful cost of war.

The words of Jesus about surrendering one's life for others did not, of course, refer to war, but they nonetheless have a particular resonance in relation to the sacrifice of those who died in two world conflicts. No doubt the motives of those who fought were many and varied, but the majority unquestionably saw themselves as defending the cause of justice and freedom, just as most in peacekeeping forces today probably still do. Whatever our feelings on the morality or otherwise of war, it is undeniable that much of what we take for granted today is down to the willingness of past generations to pay the ultimate price. We owe it to them to work for peace and so, truly, to honour their legacy.

Prayer

Loving God,
    I remember today the awfulness of conflict,
    the stark reality of war:
    how countless lives were lost or shattered in years of senseless slaughter,
    yet also how evil, hatred and injustice were overcome through courageous service
    beyond the call of duty.
Teach me to appreciate the freedom I enjoy
    and never to forget what it cost so many.
Conscious of the debt I owe,
    may I always cherish the things so many died for –
    liberty, justice and peace –
    so that their deaths will not have been in vain.
Come afresh to our broken world,
    and by your grace bring healing.
Amen.

Index of biblical passages

Old Testament

Genesis
1:26	380
2:2	224
3:9-13	184

Psalms
19:12	186
24:1; 95:4	382
26:2, 3	188
32:1-5	180
38:18	190
39:5	226
44:1, 7a	404
51:2, 7	192
69:5	194
89:1, 2	144
90:1-4, 10, 12	150
92:12-14	242
95:3-7a	384
103:8-12	196
133:1-3	168

Proverbs
1:5-7	244
14:21, 31	212
28:13	198

Ecclesiastes
3:1-8	228
4:6	230
11:7	152

Isaiah
1:18	52
9:2	98
11:6-9	70
30:15	232
40:3a	32
40:3b	34
46:9, 10, 11b	54
52:7, 8a	56
55:1, 2	246

Jeremiah
2:22	200

Hosea
6:3	248
8:7a; 10:12a	386

Micah
5:2-5a	72
7:18, 19	202

Zephaniah
1:12-16	14

Zechariah
4:6	360

Malachi
2:17–3:3a, 5	16

New Testament

Matthew
1:1-6	58
1:18-20	100
1:21, 22	60
1:21, 24, 25	102
1:22, 23	104
2:1, 2	156
2:3, 4	158
2:5b	62
2:7, 8	160
2:9, 10	162

2:11b, 12	164	1:26-35	74
3:1, 2	204	1:34, 35	106
4:1-4	206	1:38	76
5:40-42	214	1:46-49	78
6:10	64	1:51-53	80
6:16-18	216	1:54, 55	82
6:19-21	218	1:67, 68a, 72-75	84
11:2-5	36	1:67, 68	44
14:22, 23	234	1:78, 79	46
24:36, 44	18	2:1-5	108
25:31-40	20	2:6, 7	110
26:21, 22	280	2:8, 9	112
26:28, 29	282	2:10, 11	114
26:69-71	294	2:12-14	116
27:62-66	312	2:15	118
28:11-14	314	2:16	120
28:15a	316	2:17, 18	122
28:16-20	318	2:19	124
28:18, 19	362	2:25-33a	126
		2:34, 35	128
Mark		4:18, 19	66
1:4	38	9:23, 24	220, 274
1:15	22	9:26	26
4:2-9	388	9:29, 30, 32, 33	262
6:31	236	9:49, 50	170
6:45, 46	238	10:40-42	240
8:29-33	250	19:36-42	268
9:2-4	260	22:8-13	276
10:32	270	23:44, 45a	300
11:7-10	266	24:5b	320
11:15	272	24:9-11	322
13:31, 32	24	24:13-21a	324
14:22-25	284	24:22-27	326
14:32-36	286	24:28-32	328
14:51, 52	288		
15:29-32a	296	**John**	
15:34	298	1:1-3a	86
15:43-47	306	1:3b, 4	130
		1:6-8	48
Luke		1:10, 11	88, 132
1:11-15a, 18-20	40	1:12, 13	134
1:16, 17	42	1:14	136

3:16	90
12:46	92
13:6-9, 12, 14-16	290
13:36-38	292
15:13	406
16:12-15	374
19:31-34a	308
19:38-40	302
20:11-16	330
20:17, 18	332
20:19, 20	334
20:27-29	336
20:30, 31	146
21:15-17	338

Acts
1:6-11	354
2:1-4, 16-18a	364

Romans
5:6-8	304
8:26, 27	368
13:11	28

1 Corinthians
1:10	172
1:18, 23, 24	278
3:2, 3a	252
12:4-6	376
12:12, 15-20	174
13:11	254
15:35	340
15:51-53	342
15:54b-57	344

2 Corinthians
3:17	366
13:5	208

Galatians
4:4, 5	94
5:22	390
6:7-9	392

Ephesians
2:19-21	176
4:11-14a, 15	256
5:14b	346

Philippians
2:9-11	356
3:17	396

Colossians
1:3-6	348
2:20–3:2	222

1 Thessalonians
5:1-10	50

1 Timothy
2:5, 6	68

Hebrews
1:1-3a; 2:1	138
2:14a	140
12:1, 2	398
13:5	400

James
3:2a	210

1 Peter
1:3, 4	350

2 Peter
3:9, 10a, 11b, 12a, 13, 14	30

1 John
3:24b	370

Jude
v. 20	258